JAMIE OLIVER
BBQ

Photography DAVID LOFTUS

Design JAMES VERITY

DEDICATED TO

Skye Gyngell

1963 — 2025

There are many things I greatly admired about Skye Gyngell – her good heart, her deep understanding of the seasons, and her humble approach to celebrating ingredients, to name just a few. Her cooking felt effortless, though there was much thought behind it. Her dishes were both elegant and understated, with simplicity at their core. Skye was one of the matriarchs of truly beautiful, modern food, and a lot can be learnt from her. It would have been a dream come true to work with Skye in some way, but many of my Fifteen students were lucky enough to be blessed by her mentorship and employment – she believed in hope and transformation for young souls in the industry. Her love and influence will be felt for generations to come.

Contents

Introduction	6
Get ready to grill	10
Grill set-up	14
Fast & impressive	23
Skewer party	59
Salads with attitude & veg galore	86
Brunch bits	115
Epic feasts	132
Burgers & patties	180
Things that make the barbecue rock	201
Cooking sustainably & kitchen notes	230
Nutrition	236
Index	242

Embrace the seasons & get grilling!

The joy of getting outdoors, in every season, in any weather, lighting that grill and cooking in the open air is something I'd love everyone to experience. So, with this book, I want to empower you with the confidence, skills and recipes to do just that.

If you're a beginner barbecuer, you'll find that with a bit of know-how, curiosity and courage, you can craft all sorts of remarkable meals. And if you're a seasoned faithful, searching for new inspiration, I'm confident you'll find that in these pages.

This isn't a book for bravado or bluster. This is about practical skills, solid recipes and plenty of tips so you can light, tend and grill with efficiency and a calm outlook.

Grilling is a wonderfully intuitive way to cook and can bring extraordinary flavour and texture to the most humble of ingredients. Here, you'll discover how to make vegetables sing with crispness and sweet char, you'll find new wonder in delicately smoking and steaming fish, you'll meet beautiful burgers – but not as you know them – and you'll uncover an array of wonderful ways to accent, grill and serve up cuts of meat. I've also included a handful of irresistible brunch bits, and those all-important supporting-actor recipes that help to make your whole barbecue experience rock.

Cooking over flame is uplifting for the soul

It's about forging memories, nourishing gatherings and tasting something real. I truly believe that managing fire is written into our DNA somehow.

From South Africa's braais and America's phenomenal pitmasters to communal grilling in Korea. From smoky fire cooking in Japan over carbonized branches to Navajo cooking techniques, the heart of the story is the same. Cooking over fire has the ability to bring people together in a way that the latest kitchen technology never could.

Barbecuing isn't just about what's on your plate

It's a primal ritual that has the ability to stir something deep within us all. Taming flames, reading the coals and orchestrating the heat is as mesmerizing as watching a sunset blaze and fade or feeling the power of a waterfall. You have to use your intuition, to learn how to respond and react, moving things around to get the best from the grill. Once you're in the groove, you'll find it's ever so satisfying.

Mastery of fire belongs to everyone

And the magic is in realizing that the grill can be for every day of the year. Fire can warm a cold blue-sky morning or transform a rainy afternoon. Roast or braise on the barbecue, even on Christmas Day, and you'll enjoy delicious, surprising results. From meals in under 30 minutes to weekend feasts, whether it's everyday cooking or hosting friends and family, I want to help you have a stress-free experience.

So let's reclaim the grill as a gathering place for food, family, friendship, gratitude and that beautiful depth of flavour that only grilling can bring.

Welcome to the heart & art of barbecue cooking

Getting your barbecue area in order before you start cooking is key in setting you up for success

For me, the skill comes from being organized, planning ahead and understanding the core techniques and protocols that will serve you well. So, take a moment to think about what you'll be cooking and what equipment you'll need, meaning you can focus on the grilling, rather than running around in a panic looking for things!

I find it helpful to have a fold-out table, chair or crate on either side of the barbecue, one for raw ingredients and food that's prepped and ready to cook, and one for your cooked stuff, so you can keep things organized and avoid cross-contamination.

Remember, every barbecue is different, and the perfect 'set-up' is the one that makes it the easiest and the safest for you. Don't worry what it looks like – if it works, it works!

Things to consider for the prep side

- Matches and natural firelighters to get things going

- Wood chips for adding extra smokiness and depth of flavour

- Long-handled tongs to put things safely on the grill and turn them while cooking

- Gloves to protect your hands from the heat

- A chopping board and chef's knife for easy prep

- Sea salt and black pepper for seasoning

- Olive oil, red wine vinegar and water in spritz bottles, allowing you to be attentive to your food as it cooks and have control of how much you use

And over on the cooked side

- A digital food thermometer to ensure your chicken and meat is perfectly cooked
- Long-handled tongs or a spatula to remove cooked food from the grill
- Serving boards and platters ready to dish up
- Extra virgin olive oil, for finishing dishes
- Staple pantry items olive oil, extra virgin olive oil, red wine vinegar, sea salt and black pepper pop up regularly but aren't included in individual ingredients lists

It's also good practice to have to hand

- A decent grill brush to use before, during and after cooking
- A bowl of hot soapy water to keep your hands clean
- A bin or rubbish bowl to keep any waste in one place
- A fire extinguisher or fire blanket, to be safe

In terms of additional equipment, I'd also recommend the following

- A chimney starter (read more on page 16)
- Long metal or wooden skewers (just remember to soak wooden skewers before use, to prevent them burning when on the grill)
- Cast-iron pans, particularly a shallow casserole pan, a large deep pan and a small frying pan
- Enamel trays and bowls that you can put directly on the grill

Grill set-up

Charcoal, gas or electric?

I'm a big fan of cooking over fire, so a charcoal barbecue will always win out for me. Once you get to know your barbecue and get in the zone, you'll find it's easy to use and a fairly clean heat source without too much smoke. Please choose sustainably and ideally locally sourced charcoal or briquettes with no nasties. Generally, the better the quality, the longer the coals will burn for, so it's worth upgrading if you can.

Gas can be very convenient, just turn it on, let it preheat, and go, and it can be a more sustainable option than charcoal. If cooking on gas, use the temperature knobs to adjust the heat across your grill to create hot, medium and cool zones that echo the charcoal set-ups I've detailed in the book (pages 18–19). If you want to add wood chips to your gas barbecue to create smokiness, simply use a smoker box or metal tray, placed directly on the bars of the grill. Finally there are electric barbecues, which definitely seem to be on the up. They're the most sustainable option of all, and can be very helpful if you live somewhere with limited outside space.

How to light your chimney starter

With charcoal barbecuing, I really recommend using a chimney starter – it will make your grill life a lot easier. Chimneys are useful as they mean you can light your coals in an even way, but also because they light quickly. I find it easiest to remove the grill from the barbecue, sit the chimney inside over a lit firelighter, and start it there. Once the coals are glowing amber at the top, carefully tip them out and use a grill brush or long-handled tongs to drag or push the hot coals to exactly where you want them. Put the grill back over the coals, and put the hot chimney somewhere safe to cool down. Once the coals and grate are in place, I like to pop the lid on for 5 minutes before I start cooking – I find it helps the bars of the grill to heat up. Check out pages 18–19 to learn more about the different coal set-ups and why they're useful, and on each recipe in this book you'll see I've recommended the best coal set-up to use.

Using the vents for heat control

You'll see that often in recipes where you cook with the barbecue lid on, I also say to have the vents open. The vents are there to help you regulate the airflow in your barbecue – the ones at the bottom let air in to fuel the fire, and the ones at the top allow heat to escape. Having the vents open means you get a stronger heat, speeding up your cooking. Occasionally I recommend having the top vent only half open – this is generally for instances where it is helpful to keep the coals going for longer, like slow-cooked meats. Where possible – and this will vary from model to model – it's good practice to have the vents open on the opposite side to the hot coals.

Cleaning your grill

It's important to give your grill a bit of love, and that means investing in a good barbecue brush and using it before, during and after grilling to keep the bars clean and prevent whatever it is you're cooking from sticking. Don't skip this step!

Good practice for charcoal barbecuing

Once you've finished grilling, close the vents to stop the coals or briquettes burning. Next time you fill your chimney starter, knock any ash off the outside of these half-used coals or briquettes and add them in with the fresh ones to light and use again. This saves waste and a bit of money, too! Before you light the chimney, clear out any old ash from the base of your barbecue – you don't want to get a build-up there as it can block the air vents, affecting the airflow and success of your grilling.

Coal set-ups

Graduated

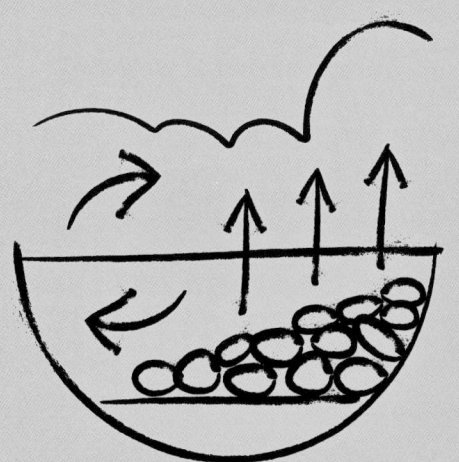

With this set-up, you want to have your coals starting high at one side, creating a fierce hot zone, and gradually sloping down to a single layer of a few coals at the other, creating medium and cool zones along the way. This allows you to have maximum control over your grilling, moving food between the zones to speed up or slow down cooking as you need to.

Flat

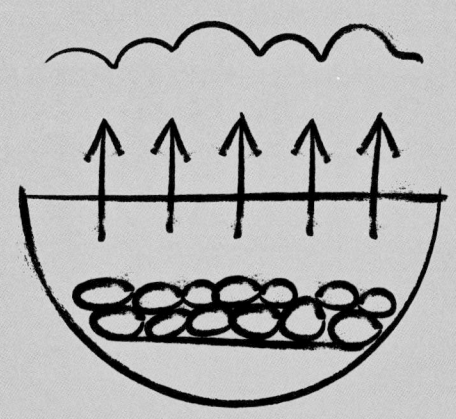

You guessed it, this is about a flat level of coals across the base of the barbecue, meaning you're ready for consistent grilling. There's no cool zone, so you need to remember to be attentive to whatever you're cooking.

50/50

Simply pile all your coals evenly into one half of the barbecue, leaving the other half clear. This gives you a clear hot zone and cool zone, with a medium area in the middle where you can get the best of both worlds. This set-up is helpful for recipes where you need to sear or get something going over direct heat, but then want to give it time to cook through more gently over indirect heat.

Channel

A channel set-up is useful when what you're cooking would benefit from more of an even all-round heat. It mimics cooking in an oven, allows you to cook at a slower pace, and is particularly well suited to lid on, vents open grilling. Arrange your coals evenly at either side of the barbecue, leaving a clear coal-free channel in the middle.

Cooking temperatures

For chicken, meat and fish, a digital food thermometer will be your best friend in working out when it's safe to eat. Simply probe the thickest part, which will take the longest to cook, and remember to wipe the thermometer clean after each use.

CHICKEN	For individual cuts like breasts and thighs, cook through to **75°C**. For whole birds, the internal temp should be **65–70°C** when you remove from the grill and needs to reach **75°C** while resting
PORK & SAUSAGES	For individual cuts and sausages, cook through to **75°C**. For larger cuts, the internal temp should be **65–70°C** when you remove them from the grill and needs to reach **75°C** while resting
STEAK	For rare, remove at **47°C**, rising to **50°C** while resting For medium-rare, remove at **52°C**, rising to **55°C** while resting For medium, remove at **58°C**, rising to **60°C** while resting For well done, remove at **65°C**, rising to **69°C** while resting
BEEF	For medium, the internal temperature should be **55°C** when you remove it from the grill, rising to **60°C** while resting, and for well done, **65°C** rising to **70°C** while resting
LAMB	For medium-rare, the internal temperature should be **55°C** when you remove it from the grill, rising to **60°C** while resting, and for well done, **65°C** rising to **70°C** while resting
FISH	The internal temperature should be **65°C** and the flesh opaque

Fast & impressive

Chicken escalope, smoky bacon, green veg & pesto

Serves 2 | 30 minutes

1 lemon

1 clove of garlic

1 bunch of flat-leaf parsley (30g)

30g shelled unsalted pistachios

1 pinch of dried red chilli flakes

30g feta cheese

4 spring onions

1 romaine lettuce

160g asparagus

160g frozen peas

2 x 150g skinless chicken breasts

2 rashers of smoked streaky bacon

1 Finely grate and reserve the lemon zest. To make a pesto, peel and finely slice the garlic, put half aside and pound the rest in a pestle and mortar with a pinch of sea salt. Roughly chop and add the parsley, stalks and all, and bash into a coarse paste. Pound in the pistachios, then muddle in 2 tablespoons of extra virgin olive oil, squeeze in the lemon juice and add the chilli flakes. Crumble in the feta and set aside (make this in a food processor, if you prefer).

2 Light the barbecue (pages 16–19). Cook the spring onions and lettuce on the hot zone until lightly charred, turning with tongs, then remove to your board.

3 Place the reserved sliced garlic in a cast-iron pan with 1 tablespoon of olive oil. Trim the asparagus and charred spring onions, then slice with the lettuce, leaving the asparagus tips whole. Add it all to the pan with a pinch of salt and black pepper and a splash of water, and cook for 5 minutes on the hot zone, or until softened, stirring regularly. Add the peas and reserved lemon zest, and carefully move the pan to the cool zone.

4 Use a sharp knife to carefully slice into the chicken breasts, then open each one out flat like a book, spritz with olive oil, season with salt and pepper, and grill on the hot zone for 7 to 10 minutes, or until cooked through, turning regularly with tongs. Crisp up the bacon on the cool zone.

5 Divide up the green veg and bacon, slice and add the chicken, then spoon 1 heaped tablespoon of pesto over each portion (stash the rest in the fridge for another day). Great with couscous, grains or crusty bread.

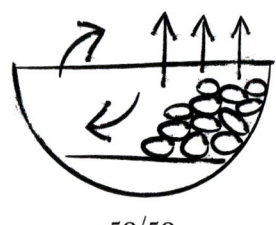

50/50

Perfect steak & chargrilled salad

Serves 2 | 20 minutes

1 x 2.5cm-thick sirloin steak (350g)

1 bunch of mixed woody herbs (20g), such as thyme, marjoram, rosemary

5cm piece of ginger

1 clove of garlic

½–1 fresh red chilli

1 tablespoon low-salt soy sauce

1 tablespoon runny honey

1 lime

160g tenderstem broccoli

160g asparagus

1 bunch of spring onions

100g radishes

160g sugar snap peas

2 sprigs of mint

1. Get the steak out of the fridge to come up to room temperature. Light the barbecue (pages 16–19). Make a herb brush by tying the woody herbs to the end of a wooden spoon with string. Peel and finely grate the ginger and garlic into a large bowl, then finely grate over the chilli. Add the soy and honey and squeeze over the lime juice. Set aside.

2. Remove the fat from the steak, discarding the sinew, then finely slice the fat and place in a small cast-iron frying pan. Put it on the cool zone to render and crisp up. Season the steak all over with sea salt. Place it on the hot zone, turning with tongs to cook gently on all sides, or until gnarly, using the herb brush to baste it with the rendered fat as you go – you'll need 2 minutes for rare (or until 47°C), 3 minutes for medium-rare (or until 52°C) and 4 minutes for medium (or until 58°C). Remove to a plate to rest – if you're using a thermometer, the temperature should go up 2 or 3 degrees as it rests.

3. Trim the broccoli, asparagus and spring onions and place on the hot zone with the radishes. Cook for 5 minutes, or until tender and charred, turning regularly with tongs and removing to the bowl of dressing once done. Trim the sugar snaps, pile into a metal sieve and place on the medium zone for 2 minutes, tossing occasionally, then add to the bowl, along with the crispy bits of steak fat, if you like. Toss well and transfer to a serving platter.

4. Slice the steaks and arrange on top, drizzling over any resting juices, then pick over the mint leaves, to serve.

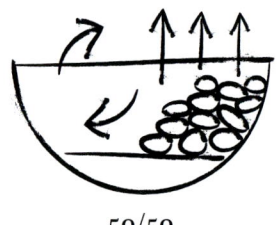

50/50

Lamb lollipops, whipped feta & pistachios

Serves 4 | **45 minutes**

200g feta cheese

3 lemons

30g shelled unsalted pistachios

12 lamb cutlets, French trimmed

1 bulb of garlic

800g new potatoes

1 tablespoon dried mint

1 tablespoon fennel seeds

½ tablespoon smoked paprika

optional: 2 sprigs of oregano

1. In a blender or a small food processor, blitz the feta with the juice of 1 lemon and 1 tablespoon of extra virgin olive oil until smooth, then season and stash in the fridge until needed. Bash the pistachios in a pestle and mortar until fine, then tip into a small bowl. Light the barbecue (pages 16–19).

2. If there's excess fat on the lamb, trim off about 2 tablespoons' worth and finely chop it, then place in a large shallow cast-iron pan on the hot zone (if you don't have any excess fat, use 2 tablespoons of olive oil). Once the fat starts sizzling, squash and add the unpeeled garlic cloves, then use a speed peeler to add the peel of 1 lemon in strips. Stir regularly until lightly golden.

3. Wash the potatoes, chop into 1–2cm chunks, and stir into the pan. Cook for 30 minutes with the barbecue lid on, vents open, or until softened, stirring occasionally and adding splashes of water, if needed. Squeeze in the juice of the zested lemon and carefully move the pan to the cool zone.

4. Meanwhile, in the pestle and mortar, pound the mint, fennel seeds, paprika and a pinch of sea salt and black pepper until fine. Scatter across your board, then turn the lamb in the seasoning until well coated. Spritz with oil, then grill on the hot zone for 10 minutes, or until golden and gnarly, turning with tongs.

5. To serve, spread the whipped feta across a platter with a drizzle of extra virgin olive oil. Add the lamb lollipops and pick over the oregano, if using. Serve with the lamb fat potatoes and lemon wedges. Use the lamb to scoop up some whipped feta, then dunk in the pistachios. Great with a simple green salad, or my Best-ever tomato salad (page 108).

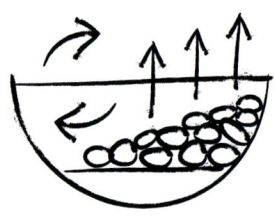

Graduated

Romesco cauliflower

Serves 4 | 35 minutes

1 head of cauliflower (800g), ideally with leaves

300g ripe tomatoes

4 cloves of garlic

100g sourdough bread

1 x 460g jar of roasted red peppers

25g smoked almonds, plus extra to serve

1 pinch of smoked paprika

4 sprigs of flat-leaf parsley

30g feta cheese

1 Light the barbecue (pages 16–19). Click off and discard any tatty outer leaves from the cauliflower, then chop it into eight wedges, spritz with olive oil, and season with sea salt and black pepper.

2 Put the cauliflower wedges and the tomatoes on the hot zone, and put the unpeeled garlic cloves on the medium zone. Slice the bread and place on the cool zone. Cook it all with the lid on, vents open, for 10 minutes, then remove the tomatoes, garlic and toast to your board. Turn the cauli and cook with the lid on, vents open, for another 10 minutes, or until charred and cooked through, moving to the medium zone if colouring too quickly.

3 Pinch off and discard the tomato skins, putting the soft insides into a blender. Squeeze in the garlic cloves and tear in the toast. Add the peppers, juice and all, along with the almonds, paprika and 2 tablespoons of extra virgin olive oil. Blitz until smooth, then season to perfection and spread across your plates.

4 Sit the charred cauliflower wedges on top of the sauce. Roughly chop and scatter over the parsley leaves and a few extra almonds, crumble over the feta and finish with a drizzle of extra virgin olive oil, if you like. Great with extra toast on the side, to mop up the excess sauce.

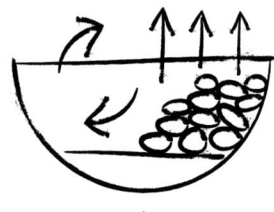

50/50

Quick beetroot mackerel

Serves 2 | 15 minutes

2 small raw beetroots (160g)

4cm fresh horseradish or 2 teaspoons creamed horseradish

2 heaped tablespoons Greek yoghurt

1 lemon

2 x 80g mackerel fillets, skin on, scaled, pin-boned

4 sprigs of thyme

1. Light the barbecue (pages 16–19) and give the grill a really good brush to clean it – this will help prevent the fish from sticking.

2. Very thinly slice the beetroots and arrange on a nice serving board with any delicate leaves. Finely grate the horseradish alongside, spoon over the yoghurt and season with a little sea salt and black pepper.

3. Halve the lemon and char cut side down on the grill. Rub the fish with olive oil and season well with salt and pepper. Pick over the thyme, then place between the hot and medium zones, skin side down, to cook for 2 minutes, or until the fish is nearly cooked through, moving it into the medium zone if colouring too quickly, then flipping over to cook through for a final minute.

4. Use tongs to squeeze half the charred lemon over the board, then sit the fish on top and drizzle with a little extra virgin olive oil, if you like. Serve with the remaining lemon, for squeezing over. Great with My favourite focaccia (page 226) or Med-style greens (page 92).

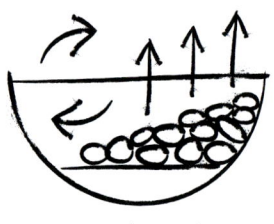

Graduated

Lemon-steamed fish & charred greens

Serves 2 | 30 minutes

Delicate white fish contrasts beautifully with the depth of flavour of charred veg in this ever-so-beautiful dinner for two. Use a flavoured mayo for an extra dimension, or go all out and make your own (page 210).

480g green veg, such as romanesco cauliflower, asparagus, spring onions, broad beans in their pods, mangetout, cabbage

2 lemons

8 chard or cabbage leaves

2 x 150g sea bass fillets, skin-on, scaled, pin-boned

1 x 50g tin of anchovy fillets in oil

optional: a few sprigs of soft herbs, such as chives, dill

4 tablespoons mayo (or make your own, page 210)

1 Light the barbecue (pages 16–19). Trim the green veg as needed, cutting the romanesco cauliflower into small florets, if using. Give it all a wash and gently shake dry, retaining residual moisture. Grill the veg until softened and lightly charred, turning regularly with tongs, and removing to a large bowl as it's done – if you have one, a wire rack placed on top of the grill will prevent smaller veg from falling through. Toss with the juice of ½ a lemon and ½ a tablespoon of extra virgin olive oil and set aside.

2 Briefly warm the chard leaves on the grill for a few seconds, then remove and spritz with water. Lay out two pairs of overlapping leaves, and sit a fish fillet skin side down on each. Spritz with olive oil and season with sea salt and black pepper, then finely slice ½ a lemon and lay it on top. Cover with the remaining leaves, then place on the grill to steam with the lid on, vents open, for 10 minutes, or until the fish is beautifully cooked through.

3 Drain the anchovies, lay them on a plate, squeeze over the juice of ½ a lemon, drizzle with extra virgin olive oil, and pick over a few soft herbs, if using.

4 Divide the dressed veg between your plates, then sit the delicately cooked fish on top, discarding the leaves. Dollop over the mayo, add a few dressed anchovies, and tuck in, squeezing over extra lemon, to taste.

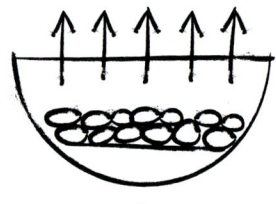

Flat

Seared carpaccio of beef

Serves 4 | 15 minutes, plus marinating

700g sirloin of beef

½ a bunch of woody herbs (10g), such as rosemary, thyme

1 teaspoon fennel seeds

½ x 50g tin of anchovy fillets in oil

½–1 fresh red chilli

2 teaspoons English mustard

3 tablespoons mayo (or make your own, page 210)

1 lemon

320g ripe cherry tomatoes, on the vine

20g rocket

1. Cut off and discard any fat and sinew from the sirloin, then place it in a small roasting tray. Strip the herb leaves into a pestle and mortar, add the fennel seeds and a good pinch of sea salt and black pepper, and pound into a paste. Muddle in 1 tablespoon of olive oil, then rub all over the meat. Cover and leave to marinate for 1 hour.

2. Lay the anchovies across a plate, drizzle with 1 tablespoon each of red wine vinegar and extra virgin olive oil, then finely slice and add the chilli. In a small bowl, mix the mustard into the mayo, then stir in squeezes of lemon juice until you have a drizzleable consistency. Light the barbecue (pages 16–19).

3. Grill the vines of tomatoes on the hot zone until softened and the skins start to split, turning with tongs and moving to a bowl once done. Sear the sirloin on the hot zone for 1 minute on each side, turning with tongs, then remove to a clean board to rest for 1 minute.

4. Use the length of a large sharp knife to very finely slice the beef, then lay the slices across your board, sprinkle with a little salt, to taste, pick over the tomatoes, add pinches of rocket and the anchovies, then drizzle over the lemony mustard mayo. Great as it is, or simply with good crusty bread.

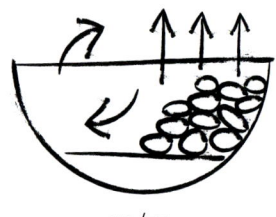

50/50

Chicken skewers & Tuscan bread salad

— Serves 6 | 40 minutes —

2 courgettes

2 mixed-colour peppers

4 x 150g skinless chicken breasts

12 bay leaves

2 lemons

8 rashers of smoked streaky bacon

1.2kg ripe mixed-colour tomatoes

1 large ciabatta loaf

1 big bunch of basil (60g)

125g ricotta cheese

1 Light the barbecue (pages 16–19). To make the skewers, chop the courgettes, peppers and chicken into 2cm chunks, discarding the pepper seeds and stalks. Place in a large bowl with the bay. Finely grate in the zest of 1 lemon and squeeze in the juice, then halve the remaining lemon, finely slice half of it and add to the bowl. Add 2 tablespoons of olive oil and a pinch of sea salt and black pepper and toss together well.

2 Load everything up on to skewers, alternating as you go, and weaving the bacon in between it all, being mindful not to pack it on too tightly.

3 Cook the skewers on the hot zone for 10 to 15 minutes, or until golden and cooked through, turning and spritzing regularly with oil and vinegar, and moving to the medium or cool zones if they're colouring too quickly. Once done, remove to a platter and squeeze over the remaining lemon juice.

4 Reserving 2 larger tomatoes, place the rest on the medium zone for 5 minutes, or until blistered and softened, turning once, then remove to a board. Halve the ciabatta lengthways and crisp up on the cool zone.

5 Halve the 2 reserved tomatoes and grate them cut side down into a large serving bowl, discarding the skin. Add 1 teaspoon of red wine vinegar and 2 tablespoons of extra virgin olive oil and season to perfection. Pick in the basil.

6 Roughly pinch off and discard the skins of the grilled tomatoes, chop the toasted bread, and toss both into the dressing. Spoon in the ricotta and gently mix together. To serve, run a sharp knife down the length of the skewers, so everything tumbles on to the platter, and get stuck in.

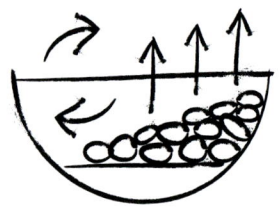

Graduated

Grilled fish tacos & stone fruit salsa

Serves 4 | 45 minutes

4 scallops, trimmed and roes removed, with the shells

50g unsalted butter, at room temperature

4 sprigs of thyme

smoked paprika, for dusting

600g stone fruit, such as apricots, damsons, plums

3 mixed-colour chillies

4 spring onions

½ a bunch of coriander (15g)

1 lime

1 x 350g trout fillet, skin on, scaled

4 x 80g mackerel fillets, skin on, scaled, pin-boned

12 small corn tortillas

4 tablespoons soured cream

1. Light the barbecue (pages 16–19). Soak a handful of wood chips according to the packet instructions.

2. Score criss-crosses into the scallops, going halfway through. Divide the butter between the shells, then top with the scallops, pick over the thyme and dust with a little paprika (if you don't have shells, use a small cast-iron pan).

3. Halve the stone fruit (leaving any damsons whole) and place cut side down on the hot-medium zone. Prick and add the whole chillies, along with the spring onions. Grill for 5 minutes, or until soft and charred, removing to a board as you go. Give the grill a good brush to clean it.

4. Halve and deseed the chillies, trim the spring onions, and finely chop it all with the stone fruit, discarding any damson stones, and the coriander, stalks and all, mixing as you go. Squeeze over the juice of ½ a lime, add 1 tablespoon of extra virgin olive oil and season to perfection.

5. Drain the wood chips and place on the hot zone. Season the trout with sea salt and cook skin side down on the medium zone with the lid on, vents open, for 5 minutes, then add the mackerel skin side down alongside, and add the scallops to the hot zone. Cook lid on, vents open, for another 5 minutes, moving the scallops to the cool zone after 3 minutes, until firm, opaque and cooked through (about another 3 minutes). Once the mackerel and trout are done, remove them to a board, then carefully pull off the trout skin and return it to the grill to crisp up.

6. Briefly warm the tortillas on the grill, then load up with the fish and scallops, stone fruit salsa, crispy skin and soured cream. Nice with lime-dressed avo and shredded cabbage, a few soft herb leaves, and some extra lime wedges.

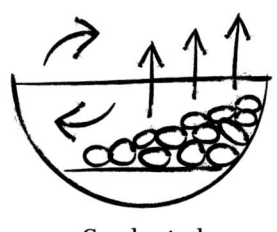

Graduated

Herby aubergine & zingy feta flatbreads

Serves 2 | 30 minutes

200g feta cheese

1 pinch of dried red chilli flakes

1 pinch of dried oregano

2 lemons

½ a bunch of mint (15g)

½ a bunch of flat-leaf parsley (15g)

20g shelled unsalted pistachios

20g baby capers in brine

1 tablespoon runny honey

2 aubergines (250g each)

2 flatbreads (or make your own, page 228)

80g mixed salad leaves

½ a pomegranate

1 Light the barbecue (pages 16–19). Soak a handful of wood chips according to the packet instructions. Place the feta in a small enamel dish, drizzle with 1 tablespoon of olive oil and sprinkle with the dried chilli and oregano, then use a speed peeler to strip over the peel of 1 lemon.

2 To make a dressing, pick most of the mint and parsley leaves into a pestle and mortar, reserving a few nice small leaves. Add a pinch of sea salt and pound into a paste, then bash in the pistachios and capers. Finely grate in the zest of the remaining lemon, squeeze in the juice, muddle in the honey and 2 tablespoons of extra virgin olive oil, then season to perfection.

3 Drain the wood chips and place on the hot zone. Prick the whole aubergines and place on the medium zone. Cook with the lid on, vents open, for 20 minutes, or until the aubergines are soft and tender, turning halfway and adding the dish of feta alongside for the last 10 minutes. Briefly warm the flatbreads, or cook through, if making your own (page 228).

4 Put the flatbreads on your plates, scattering the salad leaves on top. Slice open the soft aubergines, scoop out the flesh and spoon over the salad, then crumble over half the grilled feta (save the rest for salad, soup or wraps another day). Drizzle over the herby dressing and scatter over the reserved herb leaves. Holding the pomegranate half cut side down in your palm, bash the back so some of the seeds tumble out over the plates, then tuck in!

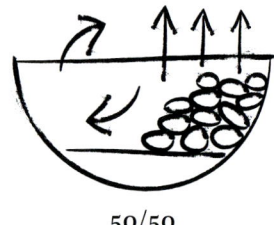

50/50

Jools' salmon niçoise

Serves 2 | 40 minutes

2 large eggs

2 teaspoons Dijon mustard

4 black olives, stone in

4 anchovy fillets in oil

½ a lemon

1 bunch of chives (20g)

400g large new potatoes

200g mixed-colour French beans

200g baby courgettes

2 x 150g salmon fillets, skin on, scaled, pin-boned

1. Lower the eggs into a pan of vigorously simmering water on the hob and boil for 5½ minutes exactly, then refresh under cold water until cool enough to handle, and peel. In a large shallow serving bowl, mix the mustard with 1 tablespoon each of red wine vinegar and extra virgin olive oil, then season to perfection. Tear in the olives, discarding the stones. Halve the anchovies lengthways, place into a small bowl and squeeze over the lemon juice. Finely chop the chives. Light the barbecue (pages 16–19).

2. Slice the potatoes lengthways 1cm thick and place on the hot zone. Trim the beans and baby courgettes and place alongside. Cook with the lid on, vents open, for 5 to 10 minutes, or until nicely charred, turning regularly with tongs, then move it all to the cool zone and cook the potatoes for a further 15 minutes, lid on, vents open, removing the beans and courgettes straight into the bowl of dressing as they're done. Remove the potatoes to a board.

3. Rub the salmon with olive oil and black pepper, then cook flesh side down on the medium zone for 8 to 10 minutes, lid on, vents open, or until golden and cooked through. Use tongs to pull off the skin and crisp it up alongside.

4. Chop the grilled potatoes into 2cm chunks and mix into the dressing bowl with the chopped chives. Quarter and add the eggs, break over the salmon, snap over the crispy skin, and finish with the anchovies, drizzling over the lemon juice they were marinated in.

Easy swap: Feel free to use regular courgettes instead – simply quarter them lengthways before cooking.

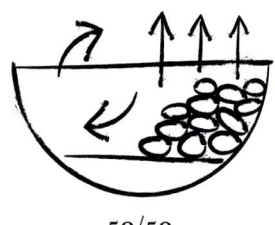

50/50

Smashed lamb wraps

Serves 4 | 30 minutes

1 red onion

2 cloves of garlic

1 tablespoon cumin seeds

1 tablespoon coriander seeds

1 x 280g jar of sun-dried tomatoes

500g lamb mince

½ a bunch of mint (15g)

1 cucumber (320g)

100g radishes

8 small flour tortillas

130g Greek yoghurt

8 pickled chillies

Embracing lahmacun vibes, these wraps are a celebration of beautifully spiced juicy lamb and fresh crunchy veg. Quick to make, but ever so delicious.

1 Peel and halve the onion, placing one half in a food processor. Peel and add the garlic, along with the cumin and coriander seeds, and a pinch of sea salt and black pepper. Drain and add the sun-dried tomatoes, and blitz until finely chopped, then pulse in the lamb until just combined.

2 Pick the mint leaves. Prep the cucumber and radishes – I've gone chunky here but feel free to finely slice, if you prefer. Very finely slice the remaining onion and scrunch with 1 tablespoon of red wine vinegar and a pinch of salt, then leave to quickly pickle. Light the barbecue (pages 16–19).

3 Divide the mince mixture between the tortillas, pressing it on and spreading it thinly to the edges. Spritz with olive oil and cook in batches, lamb side down, for 2 minutes, then flip and cook for just 30 seconds to 1 minute on the other side to lightly crisp up the tortillas. You can serve right away, or stack them on top of each other to keep warm.

4 To serve, layer up with the cucumber, radishes, yoghurt, a little quick-pickled red onion, the mint leaves and a pickled chilli. Fantastic with a generous amount of Chilli sauce (page 204), too. Roll, squash and devour!

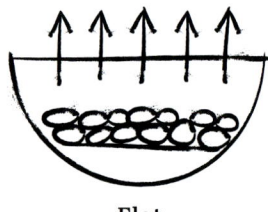

Flat

Citrus chilli tofu, greens & chickpea rice

Serves 4 | 25 minutes, plus marinating

450g firm tofu

2 tablespoons low-salt soy sauce

300g basmati rice

1 x 570g jar of chickpeas

3cm piece of ginger

1 clove of garlic

1 grapefruit

1 orange

1 lime

1 tablespoon crispy chilli oil

2 tablespoons runny honey

450g mixed green veg, such as green beans, tenderstem broccoli, pak choi, asparagus

1 Light the barbecue (pages 16–19). Cut the tofu into 4 equal slices and, in a bowl, toss with 1 tablespoon of the soy. Leave to marinate for 20 minutes.

2 Place the rice and a pinch of sea salt in a cast-iron pan with 500ml of boiling kettle water and the chickpeas, juice and all. Cook on the medium zone, with the barbecue lid on, vents open, for 15 minutes.

3 Meanwhile, to make a dressing, peel the ginger and garlic and finely grate into a bowl with half the grapefruit, orange and lime zest. Squeeze in the orange and lime juice, and mix with the chilli oil, honey and the remaining soy. Peel and segment or slice the grapefruit. Prep your chosen veg, trimming as appropriate, and halving pak choi, if using.

4 Carefully remove the rice pan from the barbecue, cover it, and leave to steam while you cook the tofu and veg. Remove the tofu from the soy, pouring any excess into the dressing, spritz it with olive oil and season with black pepper. Cook on the hot zone for 5 minutes, or until bar-marked, turning and moving to the medium zone if it's colouring too quickly – I like to brush it with a little of the dressing for the final minute. Cook the veg alongside, turning regularly until charred and a pleasure to eat.

5 Plunge the tofu and veg straight into the remaining dressing. Divide the rice and chickpeas between serving bowls, then spoon over the veg, tofu, dressing and grapefruit segments.

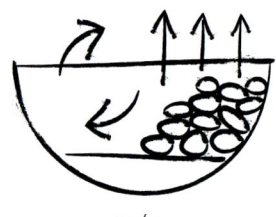

50/50

Sunshine stew & herb-stuffed sea bream

Serves 4 | 50 minutes

320g ripe tomatoes

200g new potatoes

2 aubergines (250g each)

2 courgettes

2 red onions (320g)

2 mixed-colour peppers

6 sprigs of woody herbs

3 cloves of garlic

1 cinnamon stick

1 teaspoon fennel seeds

1 tablespoon baby capers in brine

6 green olives, stone in

2 lemons

2 x 400g whole sea bream, scaled, gutted, fins removed

1 bunch of soft herbs (30g), such as flat-leaf parsley, basil, mint, fennel tops

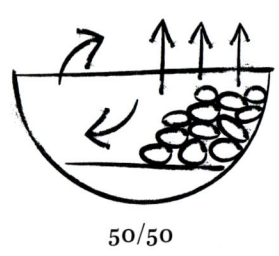

50/50

1 Light the barbecue (pages 16–19). Place the tomatoes and potatoes (halving any larger ones) on the medium zone. Halve the aubergines and courgettes lengthways, peel and quarter the onions, tear open and deseed the peppers, then grill it all for 20 minutes, or until charred and softened, turning regularly and removing to a board once done.

2 Strip and chop the woody herb leaves. Peel and finely slice the garlic. Place it all in a large shallow cast-iron casserole pan with the cinnamon, fennel seeds and capers. Destone and tear in the olives, use a speed peeler to strip in the lemon peel and add 4 tablespoons of olive oil.

3 When all the veg is off the grill, place the pan on the medium zone for 5 minutes, or until sizzling and the garlic is just starting to colour. Meanwhile, scrape away any larger bits of blackened skin from the peppers, then roughly chop with the tomatoes, potatoes, aubergines, courgettes and onions. Scrape it all into the pan, add a splash of water, and cook for 10 minutes, stirring regularly. Carefully transfer the pan to the cool zone and leave to cook until soft and a pleasure to eat, while you prep and cook the fish.

4 Slice ½ a lemon and stuff into the fish cavities with half the soft herbs. Generously season the fish with sea salt, then grill on the hot zone with the lid on, vents open, for 20 minutes, or until just cooked through – to check, go to the thickest part up near the head, and if the flesh is opaque and pulls easily away from the bone, it's done. Meanwhile, pound up the remaining soft herbs in a pestle and mortar, muddle in 4 tablespoons of extra virgin olive oil and squeeze in the juice of 1 lemon, to taste.

5 Remove the fish to a plate, let it cool a little, then use two forks to gently coax the fillets away from the fish, removing any bones as you go. Squeeze over the juice of ½ a lemon. Remove the cinnamon from the stew, season to perfection, and drizzle with a little extra virgin olive oil. Serve with the herb oil.

Chicken shawarma

Serves 4 | 1 hour 10 minutes, plus marinating

600g skinless, boneless chicken thighs

2 heaped teaspoons baharat seasoning, plus extra to serve

2 cloves of garlic

2 lemons

1 red onion

2 heaped tablespoons Greek yoghurt

1 x 425g tin of pineapple rings in juice

4 flatbreads (or make your own, page 228)

½ a small red cabbage (300g)

½ a bunch of flat-leaf parsley (15g)

320g ripe mixed-colour tomatoes

The word baharat means 'spices' in Arabic, so you can either use a shortcut shop-bought blend like I have here, or make your own mix.

1 Put the chicken into a bowl with the baharat seasoning and a pinch of sea salt and black pepper. Peel and finely grate over the garlic and the zest of 1 lemon, then peel and quarter the onion and coarsely grate over one quarter of it. Squeeze over the juice of the zested lemon, add the yoghurt, then mix and massage it all into the chicken. You can cook it right away, but it's best left to marinate for up to 1 hour, or ideally overnight in the fridge.

2 Light the barbecue (pages 16–19). Break the remaining quarters of onion apart into petals. Drain the pineapple. Take your time threading the marinated chicken, onion petals and pineapple rings across 2 long metal skewers, alternating as you go, meaning you can cook and turn them as one (getting a friend to help you here will save time!). Spritz with olive oil.

3 Place on the hot zone for 5 minutes, turning with tongs to sear all over. Move to the cool zone to cook for 30 minutes with the lid on, vents open, turning every 10 minutes until cooked through. I like to prop it against a brick wrapped in foil so you can evenly colour each of the four sides. Briefly warm the flatbreads alongside, or cook through, if making your own.

4 Use a speed peeler to shred the red cabbage, or very finely slice. Pick over the parsley, scrunch with the juice of the remaining lemon and season to perfection. Slice the tomatoes and sprinkle with a pinch of salt.

5 Slice between the skewers to help you portion up the chicken, then pile on to the flatbreads with some cabbage and tomatoes. I like to add a dollop of lemony yoghurt and a drizzle of Chilli sauce (page 204), and finish with an extra dusting of baharat. Serve leftover cabbage and tomatoes on the side.

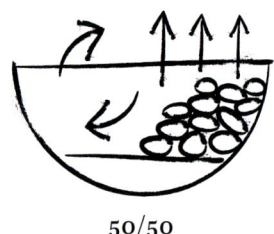

50/50

Skewer party

Chicken & chorizo skewers

Serves 4 | 25 minutes

1 red onion

2 mixed-colour peppers

2 x 150g skinless chicken breasts

75g chorizo

1 heaped teaspoon Cajun seasoning

1 lime

1 tablespoon runny honey

1 Light the barbecue (pages 16–19). Peel and quarter the onion and break into petals. Chop the peppers into 4cm chunks, discarding the seeds and stalks. Use a sharp knife to carefully slice into the chicken breasts, then open each one out flat like a book and chop into 2cm-thick chunks. Slice the chorizo into ½cm-thick rounds. Place it all in a large bowl with the Cajun seasoning, 1 tablespoon of olive oil and a pinch of black pepper and toss together.

2 Load everything up on to 4 long metal skewers, alternating as you go, and being mindful not to pack it on too tightly. Cook on the hot zone for 10 minutes, or until golden and cooked through, turning regularly, and moving the skewers to the medium or cooler zones if they're colouring too quickly. Remove and suspend over a serving bowl (like you see in the picture).

3 Squeeze over the lime juice, drizzle over the honey, then use a spoon to baste the skewers with the juices from the base of the bowl. Great served with Sriracha corn (page 94) and Charred flatbreads (page 228), with a simple slaw on the side, or as part of a bigger spread.

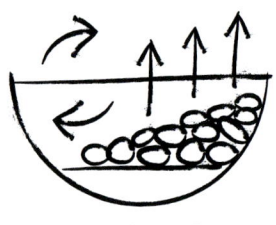

Graduated

Lamb kofta

Serves 4 | 35 minutes

1 small red onion

500g lamb mince (20% fat)

1 teaspoon garlic granules

1 tablespoon dried mint

1 teaspoon dried red chilli flakes

1 teaspoon ground cumin

1 lemon

1 bunch of mixed soft herbs (30g), such as dill, mint, flat-leaf parsley

130g Greek yoghurt

½ a cucumber (160g)

4 flatbreads (or make your own, page 228)

sumac, to serve

1. Peel and very finely slice the onion, then place in a small bowl with 2 tablespoons of red wine vinegar and a good pinch of sea salt, scrunch well, and leave to quickly pickle.

2. Put the mince into a bowl with the garlic, dried mint, chilli flakes, cumin and a pinch of salt and black pepper. Finely grate in the lemon zest, then get your clean hands in there and scrunch together well. Divide the mixture into four and, with wet hands, shape it around 4 metal skewers, using your hands to scrunch it on – a bit of texture is nice. Light the barbecue (pages 16–19).

3. Finely chop the herb leaves, reserving a few nice ones for garnish, then scrape into a bowl with the yoghurt. Add 1 tablespoon of extra virgin olive oil and a squeeze of lemon juice, mix well, and season to perfection. Use a speed peeler to peel the cucumber into ribbons.

4. Cook the kofta on the hot zone for 25 minutes, or until gnarly and cooked through, turning regularly and moving to the medium or cool zone if colouring too quickly. Briefly warm the flatbreads alongside, or cook through, if making your own (page 228).

5. Spoon the herby yoghurt over the flatbreads with the cucumber ribbons, sit the kofta on top, drain and add the quick pickled onions, and finish with a light dusting of sumac. Nice with Chilli sauce (page 204) if you like an extra kick!

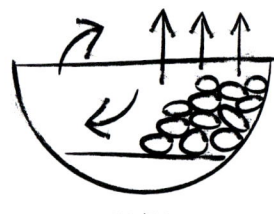

50/50

Halloumi & strawberry skewers

Serves 4 | 20 minutes

2 x 225g blocks of halloumi cheese

½ a cucumber (160g)

12 ripe strawberries

1 lemon

1 bunch of mixed soft herbs (30g), such as basil, mint, flat-leaf parsley

4 pitta breads

thick balsamic vinegar, to serve

1 Light the barbecue (pages 16–19) and give the grill a really good brush to clean it – this will help prevent the skewers from sticking. Chop each block of halloumi into six. Halve the cucumber lengthways, scrape out the seeds and chop into 8 pieces. Hull 8 strawberries. Gently skewer up the halloumi, cucumber and hulled strawberries across thin skewers, alternating as you go.

2 Finely grate the remaining 4 strawberries and lemon zest on to a platter. Squeeze over the lemon juice, add 1 tablespoon of extra virgin olive oil, mix together and season to perfection to make a dressing. Pick the herb leaves into a bowl, add a few drips of oil, and season.

3 Spritz the skewers with olive oil and cook on the hot zone for 5 minutes, or until golden and charred, turning with tongs and moving to the medium or cool zone if colouring too quickly. Lightly toast the pittas on the cool zone.

4 Sit the skewers on the platter of dressing, and serve with the herb salad and toasted pittas for satisfying scooping or stuffing. Drizzle with a little thick balsamic just before tucking in.

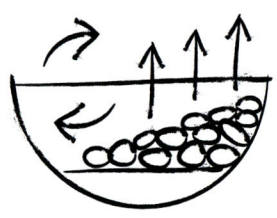

Graduated

Skewered sausages & creamy lentils

Serves 4 | 1 hour

2 cloves of garlic

1 red onion

2 sticks of celery

500g rainbow chard

6 rashers of smoked streaky bacon

½ a bunch of rosemary (10g)

1 heaped tablespoon tomato purée

2 x 400g tins of green lentils

½ x 460g jar of roasted red peppers

8 sausages

250ml single cream

your favourite mustard, to serve

1 Soak a handful of wood chips according to the packet instructions, if you've got them. Light the barbecue (pages 16–19). Peel and finely slice the garlic and onion, then trim the celery and finely slice with the chard stalks, reserving the leaves. Finely slice the bacon.

2 Put a large shallow cast-iron pan on the hot zone with the bacon, stirring regularly until golden. Strip in the rosemary, add the garlic, onion, celery, chard stalks and a very generous pinch of black pepper, and stir regularly until softened. Alongside, cook the chard leaves directly on the grill, moving frequently with tongs, and removing to a board once wilted.

3 Stir the tomato purée into the pan, followed by the lentils, juice and all. Chop up and add the wilted chard. Drain the wood chips and place on the hot zone, if using. Put the barbecue lid on, vents open, and cook for 10 minutes.

4 Meanwhile, drain the peppers and cut lengthways into strips the same width as your sausages. Skewer the sausages and peppers across 2 long metal skewers, alternating as you go, meaning you can cook and turn them as one.

5 Pour the cream into the lentils. Place the sausage skewers on the medium-cool zone, cover again with the vents open, and cook for 20 minutes, or until the sausages are golden and cooked through, turning halfway and moving them to the hot zone if they need more colour.

6 Mix up the creamy lentils, loosening with a splash of water, if needed, taste and tweak with a little mustard and red wine vinegar, then season to perfection with sea salt and pepper. Serve with the sausages and peppers, slicing down through the skewers before portioning.

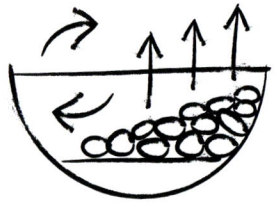

Graduated

Go veggie: Simply omit the bacon and swap in veggie sausages, adding 1 tablespoon of olive oil at the start of step 2.

Skewered sardines on toast

Serves 4 | 15 minutes

- ½ a clove of garlic
- 4 heaped tablespoons mayo (or make your own garlic mayo, page 210)
- ½ a bunch of flat-leaf parsley (15g)
- 8 x 60g sardines, scaled, gutted, gills removed
- 4 slices of sourdough bread
- 1 lemon

1 Peel and finely grate the garlic, then mix into the mayo and season to perfection. Pick the parsley leaves and toss with 1 tablespoon of red wine vinegar and a pinch of sea salt.

2 Light the barbecue (pages 16–19) and give the grill a good brush to clean it – this will help prevent the sardines from sticking. Line up the sardines on a clean worktop, alternating them head to tail. Carefully thread three skewers through them, meaning you can cook and turn them as one. Season with salt.

3 Grill on the hot zone for 2 to 3 minutes, or until beautifully charred, then turn for 1 minute on the other side, or until cooked through, moving to the medium or cool zone if they're colouring too quickly. Briefly toast the bread alongside, then line up on a board and drizzle with a little extra virgin olive oil.

4 Gently move the skewered sardines on to the toasts so they soak up all those lovely juices. Scatter over the dressed parsley, and serve with the garlic mayo and lemon wedges, for squeezing over.

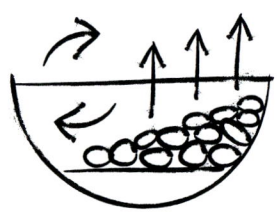

Graduated

Dr Loftus' lamb kebabs

Serves 4 | 30 minutes, plus marinating

2 lemons

1 heaped teaspoon wholegrain mustard

4 cloves of garlic

2 teaspoons each of dried thyme, dried oregano, dried basil

400g lamb neck fillet

4 rashers of smoked streaky bacon

1 onion

1 red pepper

100g button chestnut mushrooms

½ a small courgette

100g ripe cherry tomatoes

This recipe is dedicated to my good friend and photographer of this book, David Loftus. This is the dish that his dear late mum used to make for him every Tuesday when she had the afternoon off work. It's simple, it's very delicious, and I hope it becomes a part of your family's recipe repertoire.

1 Finely grate the zest of 1 lemon into a large bowl and squeeze in the juice. Add the mustard, 2 tablespoons of red wine vinegar and 6 tablespoons of olive oil. Squash in the unpeeled garlic through a garlic crusher (or peel and finely grate it), then add all the dried herbs and season generously with sea salt and black pepper.

2 Trim any sinew off the lamb, then cut into 3cm chunks. Slice the bacon a similar size. Peel the onion and cut the same size. Deseed and chop the pepper, trim the mushrooms, halving any larger ones, and slice the courgette into rounds. Add it all to the marinade with the tomatoes, mix well, then leave to marinate for at least 30 minutes, or overnight in the fridge.

3 When you're ready to cook, Light the barbecue (pages 16–19). Skewer everything up across metal skewers, alternating as you go. Cook the kebabs on the hot zone for 8 minutes, turning regularly to colour all over, then transfer to the cool zone and cook with the lid on, vents open, for another 8 minutes, or until cooked through, turning occasionally.

4 Serve with lemon wedges, for squeezing over. Delicious with yoghurt, salad and rice or flatbreads, or as part of a bigger spread.

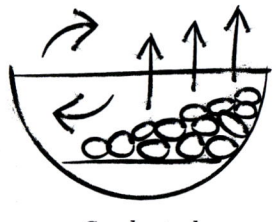

Graduated

Prawn skewers & ajoblanco sauce

Serves 4 | 25 minutes

16 large raw shell-on king prawns

120g chorizo

2 lemons

16 padrón peppers

200g blanched almonds

1 small clove of garlic

1 tablespoon sherry vinegar

½ a bunch of flat-leaf parsley (15g)

1 pinch of smoked paprika, to serve

I've embraced some of the key ingredients of ajoblanco, a delicious cold Spanish soup, to create the perfect bed of sauce for these tasty prawn skewers.

1. Peel the prawns, leaving the tails on, then run a small sharp knife down the back of each, discarding the vein. Slice the chorizo into rounds just under 1cm thick, halve and thinly slice 1 lemon, and prick the peppers. Load everything up on to 4 long metal skewers, alternating as you go, and being mindful not to pack it all on too tightly.

2. Toast the almonds in a frying pan over a medium-high heat on the hob until lightly golden (or toast in a metal sieve over the hot zone, if you've got the barbecue lit already), then tip them into a small blender or food processor. Peel and add the garlic, along with the sherry vinegar and 250ml of cold water. Season with sea salt and blitz until you have a thick, smooth paste, loosening with extra splashes of cold water, if needed. Spread on a serving platter.

3. Pound the parsley, stalks and all, in a pestle and mortar with a pinch of salt to a fine paste, then finely grate in the zest of the remaining lemon and muddle in 4 tablespoons of extra virgin olive oil. Light the barbecue (pages 16–19).

4. Cook the skewers on the hot zone for 3 to 4 minutes, or until beautifully charred and cooked through, turning regularly and moving to the medium or cool zone if they're colouring too quickly. Transfer to the serving platter, drizzle over some parsley oil, squeeze over the remaining lemon juice and finish with a nice dusting of paprika.

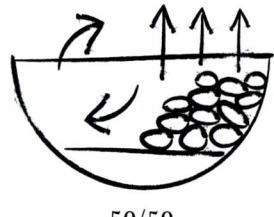

50/50

Blushing bavette skewers & ssamjang

Serves 4 | 15 minutes, plus marinating

2 teaspoons low-salt soy sauce

1 teaspoon sesame oil

1 tablespoon runny honey

1 clove of garlic

500g bavette steak

1 iceberg lettuce

400g mixed crunchy veg, such as radishes, cucumber, carrot, white cabbage

1 lime

2 heaped tablespoons ssamjang

Ssamjang is a popular Korean paste or sauce that brings big, bold flavour to all sorts of dishes, pairing particularly well with this blushing bavette.

1. Mix the soy, sesame oil and honey in a large bowl. Peel and finely grate in the garlic and add 1 teaspoon of black pepper. Cut the beef into 3cm chunks, then add to the bowl, mix and leave to marinate for at least 30 minutes, or overnight in the fridge. Light the barbecue (pages 16–19).

2. Skewer up the marinated beef, being mindful not to pack it on too tightly, and cook on the hot zone for 8 minutes for blushing, or until cooked to your liking, turning with tongs to ensure even cooking.

3. Meanwhile, click the lettuce apart into cups, then prep, shred, finely slice or matchstick the mixed crunchy veg to your liking and pile on to a platter. Cut the lime into wedges.

4. Serve the skewers with the crunchy veg and ssamjang, stuffing it all into the iceberg cups before tucking in. I like to spoon over some of the tasty resting juices, and add a squeeze of lime, to taste. Outrageously good!

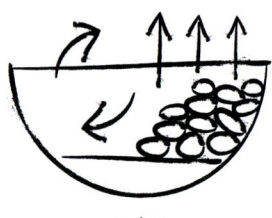

50/50

Sticky sriracha tofu

Serves 2 | 25 minutes

2 nests of instant vermicelli rice noodles (90g total)

½ a bunch of coriander (15g)

½ a cucumber (160g)

200g radishes

1 tablespoon rice wine vinegar

3cm piece of ginger

2 tablespoons low-salt soy sauce

300g firm tofu

150g shiitake mushrooms

3 tablespoons sriracha chilli sauce

2 tablespoons runny honey

20g unsalted roasted peanuts

1. Soak a handful of wood chips according to the packet instructions. Put the noodles into a bowl, just cover with boiling kettle water and leave to rehydrate for a few minutes, then drain and put aside. Pick the coriander.

2. Use a speed peeler to peel the cucumber into ribbons. Very finely slice half the radishes. Toss both with the rice wine vinegar and a small pinch of sea salt in a large serving bowl. Light the barbecue (pages 16–19).

3. Peel and finely grate the ginger into another bowl, then mix in the soy and 1 tablespoon of olive oil. Chop the tofu into 3cm chunks, halve the remaining radishes and add to the bowl with the mushrooms. Toss to coat, then thread on to skewers, alternating as you go.

4. Drain the wood chips and place on the hot zone. Cook the skewers on the medium zone, lid on, vents open, for 10 minutes, or until cooked through, turning regularly. Mix the sriracha with the honey and brush over the skewers, cooking for a couple more minutes, or until sticky and beautifully gnarly. Toast the nuts in a metal sieve alongside, removing once golden, then toss the nuts in the remaining sriracha and honey mixture.

5. Gently toss the noodles and coriander leaves with the cucumber and radishes, then scatter over the sticky peanuts. Serve with the tofu skewers.

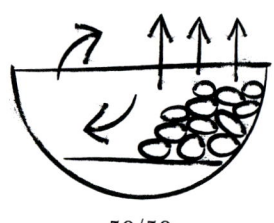

50/50

Peanutty chicken skewers

Serves 4–8 as part of a spread | 25 minutes, plus marinating

1 tablespoon ground coriander

1 teaspoon ground cumin

½ teaspoon ground turmeric

2 limes

1 x 160ml tin of coconut cream

650g chicken mini fillets

100g unsalted roasted peanuts

2 tablespoons Thai red curry paste

1 teaspoon low-salt soy sauce

½ a bunch of coriander (15g)

1 fresh red chilli

1 Put the ground coriander, cumin and turmeric into a large bowl. Finely grate in the zest of 1 lime and squeeze in the juice. Add 1 tablespoon of olive oil, 2 tablespoons of coconut cream and a pinch of sea salt and black pepper. Mix with the chicken fillets and leave to marinate for at least 20 minutes. If using wooden skewers, soak them now. Light the barbecue (pages 16–19).

2 Thread one piece of chicken on to each skewer. Pound the peanuts in a pestle and mortar until fine, then tip half into a small cast-iron or enamel pan. Whisk the Thai red curry paste with the remaining coconut cream, add to the pan, and place on the cool zone for 5 minutes, or until bubbling and reduced. Add the soy and squeeze in lime juice to taste, loosening to a saucy consistency with a splash of water, if needed.

3 Line up the skewers over the hot zone (keeping the ends of the skewers away from direct heat) and cook with the lid on, vents open, for 7 to 10 minutes, or until charred and cooked through, turning halfway and spritzing occasionally with olive oil, moving to the cooler zone if they're colouring too quickly.

4 Squeeze over the remaining lime juice, to taste, tear over the coriander leaves, then finely slice and scatter over the chilli. To serve, take a skewer, dunk it in the sauce, then dip it in the crushed nuts – delicious.

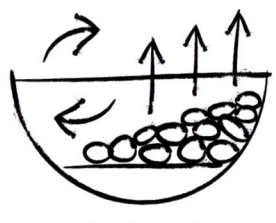

Graduated

Spiced pork kebabs

Serves 4 | 30 minutes, plus marinating

4 tablespoons madras curry paste

500g pork fillet

300g baby new potatoes

1 red onion

3 fresh green chillies

½ a bunch of mixed soft herbs (15g), such as mint, coriander

1. In a bowl, loosen the curry paste with 2 tablespoons of red wine vinegar. Trim any sinew off the pork, cut into 3cm chunks, toss into the bowl, cover, and leave to marinate for at least 30 minutes, or overnight in the fridge.

2. Cook the new potatoes in a small pan of boiling salted water on the hob for 15 minutes, or until tender, then drain and cut in half.

3. Light the barbecue (pages 16–19). Cut the onion into six wedges, then break into pairs of petals. Halve and deseed the chillies, cutting each half into two. Divide it all between four long metal skewers with the marinated pork and potato halves, alternating as you go, then spritz with olive oil.

4. Sear on the hot zone, lid on, vents open, for 7 minutes to get a nice colour, turning regularly, then move to the medium-cool zone, lid on, vents open, for another 7 minutes, or until cooked through, turning halfway.

5. Pick and scatter over the soft herbs to serve. Great with fluffy rice, cooling yoghurt and a nice stack of poppadoms.

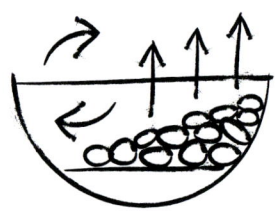

Graduated

Spiced chicken kebabs & butter sauce

Serves 4–6 | 1 hour 15 minutes

3cm piece of ginger

1 clove of garlic

1 lemon

1 teaspoon each chilli powder, ground cumin

½ teaspoon each ground coriander & turmeric

50g natural yoghurt

2 x 150g skinless chicken breasts

400g skinless, boneless chicken thighs

½ a ripe pineapple

2 small red onions

1 fresh red chilli

750g ripe tomatoes

40g unsalted cashew nuts

¼ teaspoon ground fenugreek

25g unsalted butter

150ml double cream

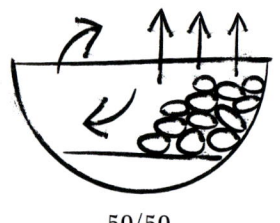

50/50

Inspired by the incredible flavours of butter chicken, here I'm serving up grilled tandoori-style kebabs with a flavour-packed sauce, fit for a feast.

1 Peel the ginger and garlic and finely grate into a large bowl with the zest of ½ a lemon, squeeze in the juice of that half, then add ½ a teaspoon each of chilli powder and cumin, the ground coriander, turmeric, yoghurt and a pinch of sea salt and black pepper. Mix together. Cut the chicken breasts into 5cm chunks and add to the bowl with the thighs. Toss to coat, keeping the breast meat and thighs separate. You can cook right away, or leave to marinate for up to 1 hour.

2 Light the barbecue (pages 16–19). Peel the pineapple and halve lengthways, discarding the core. Chop into 4cm chunks, toss with the marinated chicken breasts, then thread both on to large metal skewers. Peel the onions, cut two quarters and break into petals, then thread on to another large metal skewer with the chicken thighs.

3 For the butter sauce, chop the remaining onions into thick slices, then place on the hot zone. Prick and add the chilli and tomatoes, char it all for 10 minutes, turning regularly, then remove to a board.

4 Put a cast-iron casserole pan on the hot zone with 1 tablespoon of olive oil, the cashews, the remaining ½ teaspoon each of chilli powder and cumin, the fenugreek and the butter. Pinch off and discard the charred tomato skins, halve and deseed the chilli, then add to the pan with the onion rounds, busting up the tomatoes as you go. Season with salt and pepper, carefully transfer to the cool zone to simmer for 15 minutes, or until saucy, then pour in the cream, letting it all mingle together nicely. Remove from the grill.

5 Place the thigh skewer on the hot zone with the lid on, vents open, for 5 minutes, then add the breast skewers and cook for 10 to 15 minutes, or until cooked through, turning halfway, spritzing with oil and moving to the cooler zones if colouring too quickly. Remove and squeeze over the remaining lemon juice, then serve. Great with fresh coriander, my Coconut & coriander flat bread (page 84) a lemony crunchy veg salad, and mango chutney.

Coconut & coriander flatbread

Serves 4–6 | 10 minutes, plus resting

Tip **250g of self-raising flour** into a large bowl with a pinch of sea salt and **½ x 400ml tin of coconut milk**. Finely grate in the zest of **½ a lemon**, squeeze in the juice, then mix until it comes together. Pick and finely chop the leaves from **½ a bunch of coriander (15g)**, then use your fingertips to mix them into the dough until combined, adding a little extra flour, if needed. Knead briefly on a lightly flour-dusted surface until you have a soft dough, then oil, cover and leave to rest for 15 minutes. Use clean oiled hands to pull, stretch and flatten the dough to about 1cm thick. Grill on the medium zone for 4 to 5 minutes, or until charred, puffed up and cooked through, turning halfway and rubbing with **10g of soft unsalted butter**, and moving to cooler areas of the grill as needed.

Salads with attitude & veg galore

Charred radicchio, orange & burrata salad

Serves 2 as a main / 4 as a side | 20 minutes

2 tablespoons runny honey

2 clementines or small oranges

2 heads of radicchio or Treviso or 4 red chicory

2 heads of lettuce, such as sweetheart, round, gem

50g blanched hazelnuts

1 bunch of thyme or rosemary (20g)

1 x 150g ball of burrata or buffalo mozzarella cheese

1. Light the barbecue (pages 16–19). Mix 1 tablespoon each of honey and red wine vinegar and 2 tablespoons of extra virgin olive oil in a large shallow serving bowl, and season to perfection. Peel 1 of the clementines and finely slice into rounds, then halve the other. Trim and finely slice the base 4cm of each radicchio, then separate the leaves. Click apart the lettuce leaves.

2. Char the halved clementine, cut side down, until nicely bar-marked, then use tongs to squeeze the juice into the bowl of dressing.

3. Put a small cast-iron pan on the barbecue and toast the nuts for a few minutes, tossing regularly and removing once golden. Scatter the radicchio and lettuce leaves on the grill alongside, turning with tongs until beautifully charred and removing to the bowl of dressing as they're done.

4. Spritz the bunch of herbs with a little olive oil, then grill for 30 seconds, turning halfway so they don't catch. As soon as they're cool enough to handle, strip the leaves over the salad, then toss and scrunch it all together.

5. Add the sliced clementine, chop and add the toasted nuts, tear over the burrata, drizzle with the remaining tablespoon of honey, and serve. Great as it is, with hunks of crusty bread, or as part of a bigger spread.

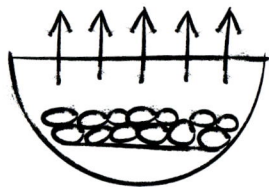

Flat

Grilled caponata

Serves 4 as a main / 8 as a side | 40 minutes

2 aubergines (250g each)

1 head of celery

2 red onions (320g)

1 lemon

600g ripe mixed-colour tomatoes

2 cloves of garlic

1 cinnamon stick

50g pine nuts

1 heaped tablespoon baby capers in brine

12 pitted green olives

1 teaspoon dried oregano

1 bunch of flat-leaf parsley (30g)

1 orange

1 Light the barbecue (pages 16–19). Slice the aubergines lengthways 1cm thick. Click away the outer celery sticks and save for another day, then halve the celery heart lengthways. Peel and halve the red onions. Halve the lemon. Put it all on the hot zone with the whole tomatoes and grill for 10 to 12 minutes, turning regularly, removing to your board when nicely bar-marked and moving to the medium or cooler zones if colouring too quickly.

2 Put 2 tablespoons of olive oil into a large shallow cast-iron pan. Peel, finely slice and add the garlic, along with the cinnamon, pine nuts, capers, olives and oregano. Place on the hot zone to fry and sizzle for 5 minutes, stirring regularly, while you chop the onion, celery and aubergines into 2cm chunks.

3 Stir the chopped veg into the pan, then spend a moment pinching the skins off the tomatoes. Mush the tomatoes into the mix, then use tongs to squeeze in the grilled lemon juice (discarding any pips). Simmer for 15 to 20 minutes on the medium zone with the lid on, vents open, or until the veg are soft, then carefully remove the pan from the grill.

4 Pick and chop the parsley, stir into the pan, season to perfection, then finely grate over the orange zest and squeeze over the juice. Finish with a drizzle of extra virgin olive oil, if you like. Great as part of a bigger spread, and a perfect treat served with grilled toasts and torn mozzarella, like you see here.

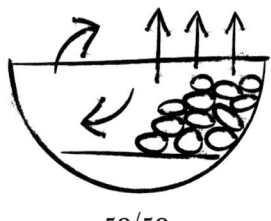

50/50

Med-style greens

Serves 4 | 15 minutes

½ a lemon

4 sun-dried tomatoes

12 mixed-colour olives, stone in

1 tablespoon baby capers in brine

500g rainbow chard

2 sprigs of basil

1. Light the barbecue (pages 16–19). Squeeze the lemon juice into a large shallow bowl with 1 tablespoon of red wine vinegar and 2 tablespoons of extra virgin olive oil. Finely chop and add the sun-dried tomatoes, tear in the olives, discarding the stones, add the capers, mix, and season to perfection.

2. Tear the chard leaves from the stalks, leaving the stalks whole but trimming away any sad ends. Give it all a wash and gently shake dry, leaving the residual moisture on the leaves. Grill the stalks in the medium zone for 2 to 3 minutes, or until lightly charred, then add the leaves for another 2 to 3 minutes, letting them wilt and steam, moving regularly with tongs.

3. Transfer it all to your board as it's done, then roughly chop and toss with the dressing. Tear over the basil leaves and serve. Delicious as part of a bigger spread, or with Arrabiatta chicken drumsticks (page 140).

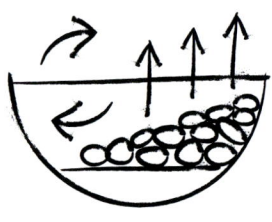

Graduated

Sriracha corn

Serves 4–6 | 15 minutes

4 corn on the cobs

2 tablespoons mayo (or make your own, page 210)

1 tablespoon sriracha chilli sauce

1–2 limes

2 spring onions

1. Light the barbecue (pages 16–19). Place the corn cobs on the hot zone for 10 minutes, or until softened and nicely charred, using tongs to roll them back and forth into the medium and cool zones as needed so you can control how quickly they colour, then remove to a board.

2. Mix the mayo and sriracha, then finely grate in the zest of 1 lime and squeeze in the juice to make a dressing. Trim and finely slice the spring onions.

3. Slice the corn off the cobs and mix with the dressing. Season to perfection, tweak with more lime juice if needed, then scatter over the spring onions. Great as part of a bigger spread, teamed with a grilled steak, or with my Chicken & chorizo skewers (page 60) or Paprika pulled pork (page 178).

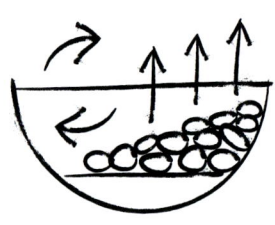

Graduated

Grilled green grain salad

Serves 6–8 as a side | 25 minutes

500g mixed asparagus, tenderstem broccoli & green beans

1 bunch of spring onions

2 fresh green chillies

2 x 250g packets of cooked mixed grains

½ a bunch of mint (15g)

½ a bunch of flat-leaf parsley (15g)

1 large ripe avocado

1 lemon

50g feta cheese

2 tablespoons pumpkin seeds

1. Light the barbecue (pages 16–19). Trim the asparagus, broccoli, green beans and spring onions, then spritz with olive oil. Prick the chillies. Working in batches, if needed, line up the veg in a grill basket for easier handling, and grill for 6 minutes, or until softened, turning halfway and charring the chillies alongside. Remove it all to your board.

2. Heat the grains according to the packet instructions, then tip into a large serving bowl. Finely chop the charred veg, leaving the asparagus and broccoli tips whole, and scrape into the bowl.

3. To make a dressing, pick most of the mint into a blender, reserving the nice baby leaves. Add the parsley, stalks and all, then halve, destone and scoop in the avocado. Scrape away the bigger bits of blackened skin from the chillies and deseed, then add to the blender with the lemon juice and 2 tablespoons of extra virgin olive oil. Blitz until smooth, loosening with splashes of water until you have a drizzleable consistency. Season to perfection.

4. Pour the dressing over the salad, gently toss to coat, then crumble over the feta, and sprinkle over the pumpkin seeds and reserved mint leaves. Delicious as it is, as part of a bigger spread, or teamed with my Pomegranate & harissa chicken (page 156) or Quick beetroot mackerel (page 32).

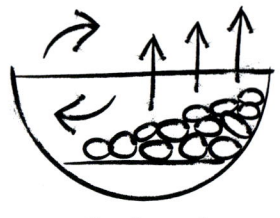

Graduated

Pickle potato salad

Serves 4–6 as a side | 30 minutes

1 small red onion

100g soured cream

100g Greek yoghurt

1 bunch of dill (20g)

8 cornichons

½ a lemon

50g feta cheese

1kg baby new potatoes

1. Peel and very finely slice the onion, place in a small bowl with 3 tablespoons of red wine vinegar and a good pinch of sea salt, scrunch together well, and leave to quickly pickle.

2. In a nice serving bowl, mix the soured cream and yoghurt together. Finely chop the dill and cornichons and scrape into the bowl with a splash of juice from the cornichon jar. Finely grate in the lemon zest, squeeze in the juice, crumble in the feta, add 1 tablespoon of extra virgin olive oil, mix well and season to perfection. Light the barbecue (pages 16–19).

3. Ideally you want all your potatoes to be a similar size, so halve any larger ones. Grill on the hot zone for 5 minutes, turning regularly until charred, then move to the medium zone with the lid on, vents open, for 15 minutes, or until cooked through. As they're done, lightly squash them, add straight into the bowl of dressing and toss well to coat.

4. Drain the quick-pickled onions and pile on top, then serve. Great warm, at room temperature or cold, and the perfect addition to any barbecue spread. It's particularly delicious with my Paprika pulled pork (page 178), Ultimate pork ribs (page 158) or Quick beetroot mackerel (page 32).

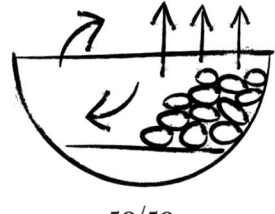

50/50

Herby grilled carrots & feta

Serves 4 | 35 minutes

750g mixed-colour carrots

2 clementines

1 tablespoon runny honey

2 tablespoons mixed seeds, such as pumpkin, sunflower, linseed

½ a bunch of flat-leaf parsley (15g)

100g feta cheese

1 Light the barbecue (pages 16–19). Wash the carrots and gently shake dry, retaining residual moisture, then halve or quarter any larger ones lengthways. Halve the clementines. Place it all on the hot zone, clementines cut side down, and cook for 10 minutes with the lid on, vents open, or until nicely charred, turning regularly with tongs.

2 Remove the charred clementines to your board, and move the carrots to the cool zone to cook for a further 20 minutes, lid on, vents open, or until tender.

3 Put 2 tablespoons each of red wine vinegar and extra virgin olive oil into a large shallow bowl. Use tongs to squeeze in the juice from the charred clementine halves, add the honey, seeds, and a pinch of sea salt and black pepper, and mix well. Pick and finely chop the parsley leaves.

4 Transfer the cooked carrots straight into the bowl of dressing, add the chopped parsley and toss well, then break over the feta and gently toss again. Delicious dished up as it is, served simply with grilled meat or grains, or alongside my Classic leg of lamb (page 144).

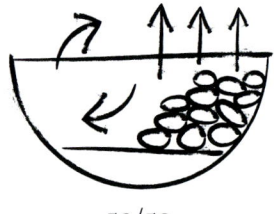

50/50

Squash, sage & rice salad

Serves 4–6 as a side | 1 hour 10 minutes

1 butternut squash (1.2kg)

300g basmati rice

50g flaked almonds

1 bunch of sage (20g)

50g dried cranberries

1 lemon

If you're barbecuing other things, this is a great one to do alongside, as you can simply leave the whole squash underneath the grill doing its thing, hands-off, then assemble this beautiful and ever-so-delicious salad to serve.

1 Light the barbecue (pages 16–19). Nestle the squash next to hot coals and let it blacken and soften for 1 hour, or until tender. Carefully remove with tongs.

2 When the squash is nearly done, place the rice and a pinch of sea salt in a pan with 600ml of boiling kettle water. Cover and cook over a medium heat on the hob for 12 minutes, or until the rice is tender and the water has been absorbed. Or, cook in a cast-iron pan on the medium zone of the barbecue, with the lid on, vents open, for 15 minutes, then remove and leave to steam with the lid on for 5 minutes.

3 Toast the almonds in a frying pan on the hob, or in a cast-iron pan on the barbecue, moving regularly until lightly golden, then remove, leaving the pan on the heat. Go in with 4 tablespoons of olive oil, pick in the sage leaves and fry until crispy, then remove to kitchen paper, reserving the oil.

4 Halve the squash lengthways and scrape out the seeds, then use a spoon to scoop all the soft flesh into a large shallow bowl, discarding the seeds and blackened skin. Add the rice, toasted almonds, crispy sage, reserved oil and dried cranberries. Finely grate in the lemon zest and squeeze over the juice, toss really well until the rice turns a beautiful orange hue and the sage is broken up, then season to perfection. Perfect as part of a bigger spread, and delicious alongside everything from simple steak to Med-style greens (page 92) or Herby grilled carrots & feta (page 100).

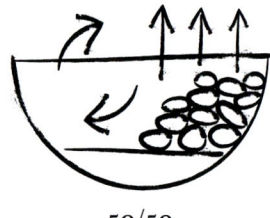

50/50

Courgette & ricotta salad

Serves 2 as a main / 4 as a side | 25 minutes

2 large ripe tomatoes

10g shelled unsalted pistachios

125g ricotta cheese

1 lemon

400g baby courgettes

2 sprigs of basil

Singing of summer, this is one of those beautiful dishes that's at its best when made with bang-in-season courgettes and tomatoes. An utter joy.

1. Light the barbecue (pages 16–19). Grill the tomatoes whole on the hot zone, lid on, vents open, for 10 minutes, or until blackened and softened. Meanwhile, crush the pistachios in a pestle and mortar or finely chop. Beat the ricotta with half the lemon juice, season to perfection and spread across a serving platter.

2. Remove the tomatoes to your board and add the courgettes to the hot zone, halving any larger ones lengthways. Grill for 12 minutes, or until softened and nicely bar-marked, turning regularly with tongs.

3. Meanwhile, scrape away and discard the bigger bits of blackened skin from the tomatoes. Quarter them and remove the core, then, in a shallow bowl, mush them up with a fork. Squeeze over the remaining lemon juice, add 1 tablespoon of extra virgin olive oil, and season to perfection.

4. Transfer the cooked courgettes straight into the tomato dressing and toss well. Pile them on top of the ricotta, spooning over any excess dressing. Sprinkle over the nuts, tear over the basil leaves, and serve. Great as it is, alongside my Classic leg of lamb (page 144), or as part of a bigger spread.

Easy swap: Feel free to use regular courgettes instead – simply quarter them lengthways before cooking.

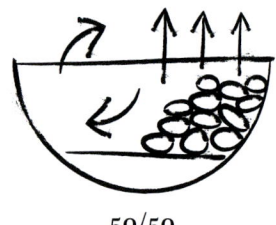

50/50

Yoghurt pasta salad

Serves 8–10 as a side | 15 minutes

500g dried pasta, such as macaroni, farfalle, shells, fusilli

500g Greek yoghurt

1 heaped teaspoon dried mint

½ a clove of garlic

1 lemon

50g blanched hazelnuts

1 heaped teaspoon fennel seeds

1 pinch of dried red chilli flakes

50g pine nuts

You get a wonderful contrast between cool dressed pasta and sizzling hot nuts in this take on macarona bil laban, a pasta dish with yoghurt sauce popular in several Levantine countries. It's a brilliant addition to any spread.

1 Cook the pasta in a large pan of boiling salted water on the hob according to the packet instructions. Drain, transfer to a large shallow serving bowl and toss with 1 tablespoon of extra virgin olive oil. Light the barbecue (pages 16–19).

2 Add the yoghurt and dried mint to the pasta. Peel and finely grate over the garlic. Finely grate the lemon zest into a small cast-iron pan, then squeeze the juice over the pasta. Mix well, and season to perfection.

3 Add the hazelnuts, fennel seeds, chilli flakes and 1 tablespoon of olive oil to the pan of lemon zest, and place on the grill, stirring regularly until lightly golden. Add the pine nuts and fry until everything is dark golden and sizzling, then pour straight over the pasta, and serve.

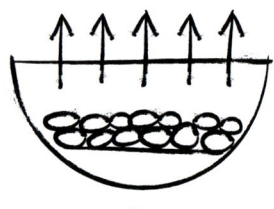

Flat

Best-ever tomato salad

Serves 6 as a side | 25 minutes

1kg ripe mixed-colour tomatoes

1 clove of garlic

½ tablespoon thick balsamic vinegar, plus extra to serve

1 x 125g ball of mozzarella cheese

2 sprigs of basil

1 Light the barbecue (pages 16–19). Soak a handful of wood chips according to the packet instructions.

2 Take the larger tomatoes (about 200g) and place on the hot zone. Put the drained wood chips alongside to impart a lovely smoky flavour. Cook with the lid on, vents open, for 10 minutes, or until the tomatoes are blackened and blistered all over. Remove and leave until cool enough to handle.

3 Pinch off and discard the blackened tomato skins, putting the soft insides into a blender. Peel and finely grate in the garlic. Add the balsamic and 1 tablespoon of extra virgin olive oil, then blitz until smooth and season to perfection with sea salt and black pepper.

4 Chop or slice the remaining fresh tomatoes, leaving any small cherry ones whole, and toss with the dressing in a nice shallow serving bowl. Tear over the mozzarella, season it, pick over the basil and finish with an extra drizzle of balsamic and a few drops of extra virgin olive oil, if you like.

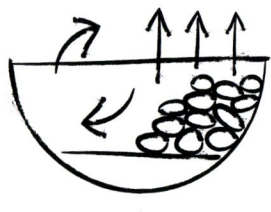

50/50

Charred squash & tahini chickpea salad

Serves 4 as a main / 8 as a side | 50 minutes

1 butternut squash (1.2kg)

2 tablespoons tahini

1 clementine or small orange

½ a lemon

1 x 570g jar of chickpeas

1 bunch of mixed soft herbs (30g), such as flat-leaf parsley, basil, mint

1 tablespoon dukkah

30g smoked almonds

1 pomegranate

100g labneh or thick Greek yoghurt

1. Light the barbecue (pages 16–19). Carefully cut the squash into quarters lengthways, then place on the medium zone and cook with the lid on, vents open, for 45 minutes, or until soft and charred, turning occasionally and moving to the cooler zone if colouring too quickly.

2. Meanwhile, put 1 tablespoon of tahini into a large shallow serving bowl, squeeze in the clementine and lemon juice, add 1 tablespoon each of red wine vinegar and extra virgin olive oil and mix well. Drain and stir in the chickpeas, pick, roughly chop and add most of the herb leaves, reserving a few nice ones for garnish, and the dukkah. Finely chop the almonds.

3. Remove the charred squash to your board, scrape away and discard the seeds, then slice 1cm thick and toss through the tahini chickpeas. Season to perfection. Halve the pomegranate and, holding one half cut side down in your palm, bash the back so the seeds tumble out over the salad. Gently toss together. Dollop over the labneh, drizzle over the remaining tahini, scatter over the chopped almonds and reserved herb leaves, and serve, adding extra pomegranate seeds and a drizzle of extra virgin olive oil, if you like.

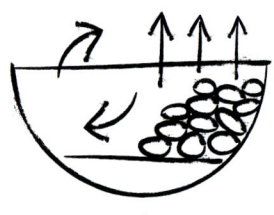

50/50

Beautiful Georgian-style stuffed aubergines

Serves 4–8 as part of a spread | 35 minutes

2 large aubergines (400g each)

100g shelled walnut halves

½ a clove of garlic

½ teaspoon ground turmeric

½ teaspoon fenugreek powder, blue if you can get it

100ml good-quality sunflower oil

1 lemon

50g feta cheese

4 sprigs of tarragon

1 pomegranate

200g Greek yoghurt

I was introduced to nigvziani badrijani, a popular stuffed aubergine dish, by Georgian chef Guram Baghdoshvili. It's traditionally eaten cold or at room temperature, but aubergine is so good grilled that I had to include this.

1. Slice the aubergines lengthways ½cm thick then, in a single layer, sprinkle generously with sea salt, and cover with kitchen paper and something heavy.

2. To make the stuffing, bash the walnuts in a pestle and mortar with the peeled garlic, turmeric and fenugreek until fine, then muddle in the sunflower oil to make a paste. Set up a fine sieve over a bowl, spoon in the paste, and push it through the sieve, capturing the golden oil in the bowl below. Set the oil aside and scrape the paste back into the mortar. Muddle in half the lemon juice and most of the feta. Pick and finely chop half the tarragon leaves, then stir through. Halve the pomegranate and, holding one half cut side down in the palm of your hand, bash the back with a spoon so all the seeds tumble out into the mortar, reserving the other half. Light the barbecue (pages 16–19).

3. Pat the aubergine slices dry, brush with a little olive oil, then grill on the hot zone for 5 minutes, or until softened and lightly charred, turning halfway – you may need to work in batches. Remove to a board and spread over the stuffing, then roll up and double skewer across 2 long metal skewers. Rub with 1 tablespoon of olive oil, season with salt and spritz with red wine vinegar. Cook for 8 minutes on the hot zone, turning regularly and moving to the cooler zone if they're colouring too quickly.

4. Hold the remaining pomegranate half cut side down in the palm of your hand and bash the back with a spoon so all the seeds tumble out into a bowl. Mix the yoghurt with the remaining lemon juice, season, and spread it across a serving board. Sit the aubergines on top, then cut between the skewers and remove them. Drizzle over 1 tablespoon of the golden oil (save the rest for salads, grilled meats and fish), pick over the remaining tarragon, scatter over the pomegranate seeds and crumble over the remaining feta.

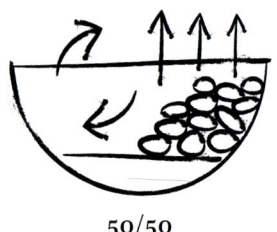

50/50

Brunch bits

Glazed rum pineapple

Serves 4 | 30 minutes

40g unsalted roasted peanuts

1 ripe pineapple

2 limes

50g unsalted butter

50ml spiced rum

3 tablespoons runny honey

optional:
1 bunch of thyme (20g)

4 tablespoons Greek or coconut yoghurt

1 Light the barbecue (pages 16–19). Crush the peanuts in a pestle and mortar, toast them in a small cast-iron frying pan on the hot zone until golden, then tip into a bowl, removing the pan from the heat.

2 Top and tail the pineapple, then slice the peel off the sides. Cut it in half through the middle. Finely grate the lime zest and put most of it into the pan, reserving a little for garnish, then squeeze in the juice and add the butter.

3 Grill the pineapple halves on the hot zone for 20 to 25 minutes, turning regularly with tongs until golden and caramelized, moving them to the medium and cool zones as needed to control how quickly they colour.

4 Place the pan on the medium zone until the butter has melted, is starting to smell nutty and looks foamy. Add the rum, flame it if you like (stand back!), then stir in the honey and use the mixture to glaze the pineapple as it cooks – I like to use a bunch of thyme as a brush for bonus fragrance. Toss the toasted nuts into the residual glaze in the pan for the last minute.

5 Spread the yoghurt over a serving platter, move the pineapple to a board and clank it up, removing and discarding the core, then pile on to the platter, spoon over the sticky nuts and sprinkle with the reserved lime zest.

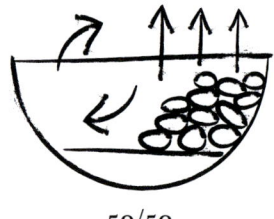

50/50

Ultimate barbecue brekkie

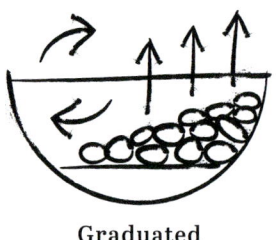

Graduated

You can either go all out and cook up every recipe on these pages, creating an ultimate breakfast feast – and I've tried it, so trust me, it really does all fit on a regular grill. Or, you can pick and choose whichever elements excite you to make up your own perfect brekkie – I also like to include a few corn (page 124) or halloumi fritters (page 130), like you see in the picture. Everything can be easily scaled up or down depending on how many hungry mouths you're feeding. And obviously, if you're cooking for veggie friends, it's polite to get the veggie stuff on the grill first, then follow up with the meat when it's done. Have fun!

Crispy bacon & sizzling sausages

Serves 4 | 25 minutes

Light the barbecue (pages 16–19). Line up **4 sausages**. Peel and quarter **1 small red onion**, break apart into petals, and poke the petals in between the sausages with the leaves from **2 sprigs of sage**. Carefully poke two long metal skewers through all the sausages, meaning you can cook and turn them as one. Take **8 rashers of thick-cut smoked streaky bacon** and thread the end of each rasher on to another long metal skewer so it dangles like a flag. Cook it all on the hot zone for 2 minutes, or until nicely coloured, moving the sausage skewers to the cool zone to cook through for 20 minutes, turning halfway, and laying the bacon on top to prevent it getting too crispy.

Go veggie: Simply ditch the bacon, and swap in your favourite veggie sausages, spritzing regularly with olive oil as they cook.

Dotty coddled egg peppers

Serves 4 | 30 minutes

Light the barbecue (pages 16–19). Halve and deseed **2 peppers**, leaving the stalks attached for easier handling. Grill cut side down on the hot zone with the lid on, vents open, for 15 minutes, or until starting to soften, adding **100g of ripe cherry tomatoes on the vine** to cook alongside for the last 5 minutes. Flip the peppers, then season with a little sea salt and black pepper. Take **4 eggs** and crack one into each pepper half, divide the tomatoes between them, then spritz with olive oil. Cook on the hot zone with the lid on, vents open, for 10 to 15 minutes, or until the peppers are soft and the eggs are cooked to your liking, carefully moving to the medium zone if they're colouring too quickly.

Tomato bread

Serves 4 | 20 minutes

Light the barbecue (pages 16–19). Place **200g of ripe cherry tomatoes on the vine** on the medium zone to cook with the lid on, vents open, for 5 minutes, or until softened and charred. Grill **2 thick slices of sourdough bread** on the cool zone until lightly toasted on each side, then remove. Halve **1 clove of garlic** and rub each hot toast once with the cut side, then drizzle with extra virgin olive oil. Use tongs or a fork to smush and rub the soft tomatoes on to both sides of the bread, discarding the vines. Return to the grill (or cast-iron pan, if using for other things) on the hot zone until wonderfully gnarly on each side, moving to the cooler zone if colouring too quickly. Slice, and serve.

Bubbling baked beans

Serves 4 | 15 minutes

Light the barbecue (pages 16–19). Simply open **2 x 400g tins of baked beans** and sit them on the cool zone. Let them bubble away while the rest of your brekkie cooks, carefully stirring occasionally, until hot through and bubbling. Carefully remove the hot tins from the grill and season to perfection with dashes of **Worcestershire and Tabasco sauce**.

Stuffed mushrooms

Serves 4 | 25 minutes

Light the barbecue (pages 16–19) and preheat a cast-iron pan on the cool zone. Trim **4 portobello mushrooms**, then grill on the hot zone, cup side down, with the lid on, vents open, for 10 minutes, or until softened. Very finely slice, then roughly chop **100g of halloumi cheese**. Finely grate over the zest of **½ a lemon**, tear over the leaves from **2 sprigs of basil**, drizzle with 1 teaspoon of olive oil, season with black pepper and scrunch together. Flip the mushrooms, season, transfer them to the hot skillet, then divide the halloumi mixture between them. Carefully move the pan to the hot zone and cook with the lid on, vents open, for 10 to 15 minutes, or until melty and delicious, carefully moving the skillet to the medium zone if they're colouring too quickly.

Corn fritters

— Serves 4 | 25 minutes —

100g fresh or tinned sweetcorn

100g cottage cheese

100g coarse cornmeal

100g self-raising flour

40ml semi-skimmed milk

½ teaspoon baking powder

2 large eggs

30g jarred sliced jalapeños

1 ripe avocado

1 lime

3 ripe mixed-colour tomatoes

2 sprigs of basil

4 tablespoons Greek yoghurt

chilli oil or chilli jam, to serve

1. Put the sweetcorn into a large bowl (drain first, if using tinned) with the cottage cheese, cornmeal, flour, milk and baking powder. Crack in the eggs and add the jalapeños, along with 3 tablespoons of juice from the jar. Add 3 tablespoons of olive oil, season with sea salt and black pepper, and mix well. Light the barbecue (pages 16–19). Preheat a cast-iron pan on the cool zone.

2. Carefully move the pan to the hot zone, spritz with oil and, in batches or to order, cook tablespoons of the batter – about 4 to 5 per person – for 2 to 3 minutes on each side, or until golden and cooked through, carefully moving the skillet to the medium zone if they're colouring too quickly.

3. Meanwhile, halve, destone, peel and slice the avo, then dress with lime juice and season to perfection. Finely slice the tomatoes. Divide it all between your plates, tear over the basil leaves and dollop over the yoghurt. Pile the fritters on top and drizzle with chilli oil. This is wonderful in its own right, but also makes a lovely addition to my Ultimate barbecue brekkie (pages 118–123).

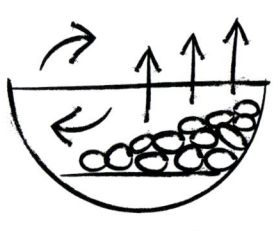

Graduated

BBQ baked beans

Serves 8–10 | 45 minutes

½ x Store-cupboard BBQ sauce (page 202)

2 cloves of garlic

1 x 460g jar of roasted red peppers

1 bunch of sage (20g)

500g fresh or frozen chopped mixed onion, carrot & celery

1 x 400g tin of cherry tomatoes

2 x 400g tins of mixed beans

1. Make the Store-cupboard BBQ sauce (page 202). Peel and finely slice the garlic. Drain and finely chop the peppers. Light the barbecue (pages 16–19).

2. Put a large deep cast-iron pan over the hot zone with 2 tablespoons of olive oil, and pick in the sage leaves. Fry until crispy, then use tongs or a slotted spoon to remove half to a plate lined with kitchen paper for later.

3. Go in with the garlic, stirring regularly, and, once lightly golden, add the chopped mixed veg. Cook for 5 to 10 minutes, or until starting to colour, then tip in the tomatoes, breaking them up with your spoon. Add the chopped peppers, the beans, juice and all, and the BBQ sauce. Once it starts bubbling, carefully move to the medium zone and simmer with the barbecue lid on, vents open, for 30 minutes, or until thickened, stirring occasionally.

4. Season the beans to perfection with sea salt and black pepper, and serve sprinkled with the reserved crispy sage. Great with fresh bread, grilled toasts, or piled on to tortillas or tacos. Lovely with a fried egg, or you could even crack some eggs into the beans to coddle for the last few minutes. Also a dream dished up with my Ultimate barbecue brekkie (pages 118–123).

Helpful hint: If you don't have the barbecue lit for other things, you can absolutely cook this inside on the hob, if you prefer.

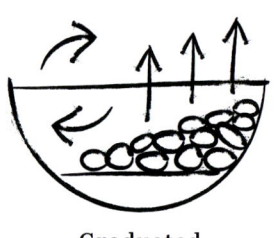

Graduated

Grilled black pepper peaches

Serves 4 | 20 minutes

250g ricotta cheese

2 tablespoons runny honey

1 lemon

4 ripe peaches

4 slices of panettone or brioche (300g)

1. Put the ricotta and honey into a bowl and beat until smooth. Finely grate over the lemon zest and beat again until you have a whipped consistency. Halve and destone the peaches. Light the barbecue (pages 16–19).

2. Spritz the peach halves with olive oil, then grill on the hot zone until beautifully charred, turning with tongs. Move them to the medium-cool zone and cook for 10 minutes with the lid on, vents open, or until softened.

3. Briefly toast the panettone slices on the hot zone, then remove to serving plates and top with the grilled peaches. Spoon over the whipped ricotta and season with a generous pinch of black pepper (trust me!). Finish with a little squeeze of lemon and a few drips of extra virgin olive oil, if you like.

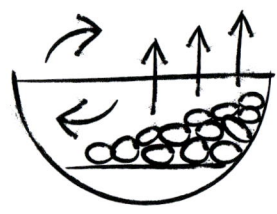

Graduated

Halloumi fritters

Serves 6 | 40 minutes

2 large eggs

250g self-raising flour

150ml semi-skimmed milk

12 mixed-colour olives, stone in

1 cucumber (320g)

250g watermelon

1 lemon

1 fresh red chilli

4 spring onions

200g halloumi cheese

1 bunch of mint (30g)

1 Light the barbecue (pages 16–19). In a large bowl, whisk the eggs into the flour with a pinch of sea salt, then gradually whisk in the milk until smooth.

2 For the salsa, squash and destone the olives, then finely chop. Roughly peel the cucumber with a speed peeler, halve it lengthways and use a teaspoon to scrape out the seedy core, then chop into 1cm chunks. Peel and dice the watermelon into 1cm chunks. Scrape it all into a bowl, ready to dress later.

3 Finely slice the lemon, prick the chilli, trim the spring onions, then place it all on the hot zone with the block of halloumi. Use tongs to turn it all until lightly charred, removing it to your board as it's done. Finely chop the lemon, chop up the spring onions, scrape the skin off the chilli, deseed and finely slice it, and clank up the halloumi. Scrape it all into the bowl of batter, pick, roughly chop and add most of the mint leaves, and mix together.

4 Put a large shallow cast-iron pan on the medium-hot zone. Spritz with olive oil and add spoonfuls of batter, spreading them out to about 2cm thick. Cook for 3 minutes on each side, or until dark golden and cooked through, moving to the cool zone of the grill to keep warm while you cook the rest.

5 Pick the remaining mint leaves into the salsa, toss it all with 1 tablespoon each of red wine vinegar and extra virgin olive oil, and season to perfection. Chop up the fritters and serve with the salsa. Great with a fried egg, or on a bed of natural yoghurt swirled with Chilli sauce (page 204).

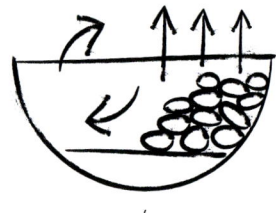

50/50

Epic feasts

Barbecued meat chilli

Serves 12 | 3 hours

1 teaspoon cumin seeds

4 cloves of garlic

1 x 95g jar of chipotle chilli paste

6 large chicken thighs, skin on, bone in (800g)

800g piece of pork shoulder, fat trimmed

800g skirt steak

3 mixed-colour peppers

6 fresh jalapeño chillies

4 sticks of celery

1 bunch of spring onions

3 x 400g tins of plum tomatoes

800ml hot coffee

1 x 570g jar of butter beans

½ a bunch of coriander (15g)

1. Light the barbecue (pages 16–19) and soak a handful of wood chips according to the packet instructions. In a pestle and mortar, pound the cumin seeds with 2 teaspoons each of sea salt and black pepper until fine. Peel and pound in the garlic, then muddle in the chilli paste. Put the chicken, pork and steak into a large deep cast-iron pan, add the chilli paste mixture, and massage well.

2. Prick the peppers and chillies, then lightly char over the medium zone with the celery and spring onions, removing to your board once nicely bar-marked.

3. Place all the meat directly on the hot or medium zone for 10 minutes, or until seared all over, turning regularly with tongs, while you trim and slice the spring onions and celery, halve and deseed the chillies, and roughly chop the peppers, discarding the seeds and stalks.

4. Scrape the veg into the empty pan and place on the medium zone. Add the seared meat, then tip in the tomatoes and pour in the coffee. Cover the pan, then put the barbecue lid on, top vent half open, and cook for 2 hours – the temperature of the barbecue should sit at around 180°C.

5. Carefully remove the pan lid, then stir in the beans, juice and all. Drain the wood chips and place on the hot zone. Cook lid on, vents open, for 30 minutes, then stir well and check that all the meat is falling off the bones.

6. Shred all the meat, discarding the chicken bones and skin. Finely chop and stir in the coriander leaves with 1 tablespoon of red wine vinegar, then season to perfection. Great served with rice, yoghurt, Chilli sauce (page 204) and chunks of lime-dressed avo, if you fancy.

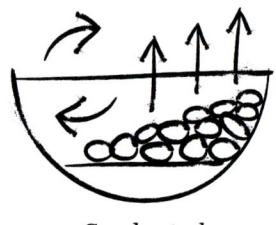

Graduated

Helpful hint: Fill the empty chipotle chilli paste jar with olive oil, give it a good shake and you can use it to add bonus flavour to all sorts of dishes!

Juicy pork belly, fennel & orange salad

Serves 10 | Prep 10 minutes | Cook 5 hours, plus resting

2kg piece of pork belly, skin on, bone in

1 big bunch of mixed woody herbs (60g), such as oregano, marjoram, sage, thyme, rosemary

2 lemons

2 firm pears

1 bulb of fennel

2 sticks of celery

2 oranges

100g black olives, stone in

1 fresh red chilli

1 Light the barbecue (pages 16–19). Place a roasting tray with 400ml of water underneath the grill in the cool zone – this will help the pork steam and you'll capture beautiful juices.

2 Use a skewer or sharp knife to stab all over the skin of the pork belly (don't score it, as that will release too much fat). Rub all over with 2 teaspoons of sea salt, getting it into the holes, then place over the hot zone for 5 minutes, or until golden brown all over, turning regularly with tongs. Remove to a board.

3 Strip half the herb leaves into a pestle and mortar and pound to a paste. Muddle in the juice of ½ a lemon, reserving the squeezed half, and 4 tablespoons of olive oil, then pour over and massage into the pork.

4 Place the pork skin side down on the cool zone. Rub the remaining herb sprigs in the leftover herb oil on the board and tuck them, along with the squeezed lemon half, under the side of the pork closest to the coals to protect it as it cooks. Cook for 5 hours with the lid on, top vent half open, or until gnarly and meltingly tender, checking occasionally and topping up the tray with more water if it looks dry. The barbecue temperature should start at around 240°C, then you want it to settle between 180°C and 200°C for another 1½ to 2 hours, then it will continue to drop to about 150°C. Once cooked, remove the pork, then carefully remove the grill and the tray of juices. Sit the pork in the tray to rest for 30 minutes.

5 To make a fresh, delicate salad, very finely slice the pears, fennel (reserving any leafy tops) and celery with a speed peeler or good knife skills. Peel the oranges and finely slice into rounds. Squeeze over the juice of 1 lemon, add 1 tablespoon of extra virgin olive oil, gently toss together, then season to perfection and spread across a serving platter. Squash, destone and finely chop the olives with the chilli (deseed, if you like), then dress in ½ a tablespoon of extra virgin olive oil and the remaining lemon juice.

6 Slice the pork and lay on the salad, spooning over any resting juices. Sprinkle over the chopped olives and any reserved fennel tops. It's worth the wait!

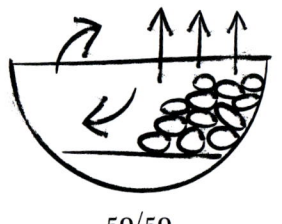

50/50

Gnarly rump steak with salsa, rice & beans

Serves 10 | Prep 15 minutes | Cook 50 minutes, plus resting

2 red onions

75g chorizo

500g basmati rice

6 bay leaves

1 x 400g tin of cannellini beans

1.5kg piece of rump steak

½ a bunch of rosemary (10g)

½ a ripe pineapple (400g) or 1 x 432g tin of pineapple in juice

2 red peppers

450g ripe tomatoes

½ a bunch of mint (15g)

120g rocket

1. Light the barbecue (pages 16–19). Peel and finely chop ½ an onion, reserving the rest, finely chop the chorizo, then place it all in a cast-iron casserole pan with the rice and bay. Tip in the beans, juice and all, along with 1½ tins' worth of water and a pinch of sea salt. Stir well.

2. Score the fat on top of the steak in a criss-cross pattern to help it render quickly. Season generously with salt and black pepper, then place on the medium zone with the rosemary sprigs underneath. Colour for 10 minutes in total, turning occasionally with tongs, until coloured on all sides – if it flares up, carefully move to the cooler zone.

3. Carefully remove the grill and place the rice pan directly in the cool zone. Replace the grill, then sit the steak fat side down on the bars, over the pan. Cook with the lid on, top vent half open above the meat for 40 to 50 minutes for blushing medium-rare – the internal temperature should be 55°C.

4. Meanwhile, peel and finely dice the remaining onions and the pineapple and scrape on to a serving platter big enough for the beef. Deseed and finely dice the peppers, finely dice the tomatoes and add it all to the platter, then pick, finely chop and add the mint leaves. Dress with 1 tablespoon each of red wine vinegar and extra virgin olive oil and season to perfection.

5. Rest the steak on top of the salsa for at least 30 minutes – the internal temperature should reach 60°C. Carefully remove the rice pan, and cover until serving. Slice the steak 1cm thick, drizzle with a little extra virgin olive oil and season with salt. Serve with the salsa, rice and beans, and the rocket.

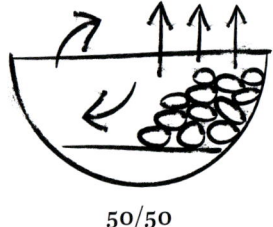

50/50

Arrabiatta chicken drumsticks

Serves 6 | 1 hour 15 minutes

4 cloves of garlic

2 large onions

6 fresh red chillies

12 chicken drumsticks

4 bay leaves

90g smoked bacon lardons

1 lemon

1kg ripe tomatoes

2 tablespoons tomato purée

100ml vodka

1. Light the barbecue (pages 16–19). Peel and slice the garlic cloves. Peel and halve the onions. Prick the chillies. Drizzle the chicken with 1 tablespoon of olive oil and season with sea salt and black pepper.

2. Put a large shallow cast-iron pan on the medium zone with 1 tablespoon of oil, the garlic, bay and lardons. Use a speed peeler to add the lemon peel in strips, and fry it all until lightly golden, stirring regularly.

3. Alongside, grill the halved onions, whole chillies and tomatoes for 8 to 10 minutes, or until softened and nicely bar-marked, then remove to a board. Adding to the pan as you go, chop the onions into rough 1cm chunks, squash or clank up the tomatoes, and deseed, slice and add the chillies, scraping away the larger bits of blackened skin. Stir in the tomato purée.

4. Grill the chicken drumsticks on the hot zone for 10 minutes, or until golden all over, turning regularly with tongs, then nestle them into the pan. Add the vodka and flame it, if you like (stand back!). Squeeze in the lemon juice, then cook with the lid on, vents open, for 45 minutes, or until the chicken is cooked through. Great with a side salad, and rice, couscous or hunks of crusty bread to mop up all those delicious juices.

Epic chicken arrabiatta sarnie

Make **My favourite focaccia** (page 226), halve it through the middle, and you can use this dish to make the most epic of epic sarnies! Simply shred all the meat, discarding the bones, then spread the arrabiatta sauce across the base of the focaccia, piling the meat on top. Sprinkle over a layer of **rocket**, tear over **1 x 125g ball of mozzarella cheese**, use a speed peeler to add a few shavings of **Parmesan cheese**, then sandwich together, slice and serve. I like to finely grate over a bit of extra Parmesan for a fancy finish, too. Great for 12 very lucky people. Check the pictures on the following pages for inspo!

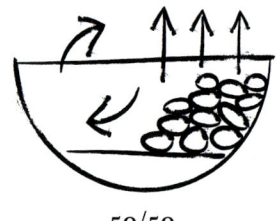

50/50

Classic leg of lamb

Serves 10 | Prep 10 minutes | Cook 1 hour 15 minutes, plus resting

3kg leg of lamb, bone in, French trimmed (ask your butcher)

6 cloves of garlic

2 large lemons

1 bunch of sage (20g)

1 x 50g tin of anchovy fillets in oil

6 large red onions

1kg ripe mixed-colour tomatoes

1. Use a small sharp knife to make 6 deep incisions into each side of the lamb (12 in total), poking your finger into each to make little pockets.

2. Peel and halve the garlic. Use a speed peeler to strip off 12 pieces of lemon peel. Pick and lay out 12 big sage leaves, then divide the halved garlic, anchovies and lemon peel between them. Drizzle with the oil from the anchovy tin, then roll up each stack and stuff into the pockets in the lamb. Season all over with sea salt and black pepper. Light the barbecue (pages 16–19).

3. Halve the unpeeled onions through the root. Sit the lamb in the centre of the grill with the onion halves snugly around it, cut side up. Cook with the lid on, top vent half open, for 1 hour 15 minutes, or until the internal temperature reaches 55°C, checking after 1 hour. Transfer to a plate with the onions and leave to rest, covered, for 30 minutes (the internal temp should rise to 60°C).

4. Finely slice the tomatoes and arrange over a large serving board. Pinch the skins off the soft onions, add to the board, then sit the lamb on top. Pour over any resting juices, squeeze over the lemon juice, carve, and serve. Cute with a few chive flowers over the top, if you've got them. Delicious with a multitude of things, including my Grilled caponata (page 90), Med-style greens (page 92) or Salsa verde (page 206). Enjoy!

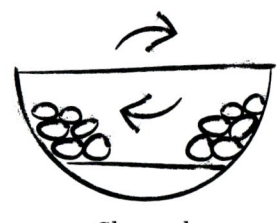

Channel

Herby grilled veg, halloumi skewers & pancakes

Serves 8 | 45 minutes, plus resting

300g strong bread flour

1 x 7g sachet of dried yeast

2 tablespoons runny honey

1 large aubergine (400g)

2 courgettes

1 red onion (160g)

2 red peppers (320g)

1 bulb of fennel

200g ripe mixed-colour cherry tomatoes

150g mixed unsalted nuts

1 clove of garlic

50g dried cranberries

1 bunch of mixed soft herbs (30g)

200g halloumi cheese

2 mixed-colour chillies

1 lemon

100g Greek yoghurt

½ a pomegranate

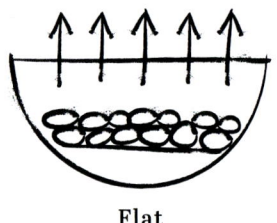

Flat

1. Light the barbecue (pages 16–19). Tip the flour into a bowl, add 1 teaspoon of sea salt and the yeast, then whisk in 500ml of lukewarm water, the honey and 2 tablespoons of olive oil. Cover and leave for 30 minutes to do its thing (near the warmth of the barbecue is great!) – it should be aerated and bubbly.

2. Slice the aubergine and courgettes ½cm-thick lengthways. Peel the onion and slice into ½cm rounds. Cut the peppers into similar-sized chunks, discarding the seeds and stalks. Halve the fennel lengthways, then cut into 1cm-thick wedges, reserving any leafy tops. Working in batches, grill all the veg with the tomatoes for 4 minutes, or until softened and charred, turning halfway, and removing to a board once done.

3. For the dressing, blitz the nuts, peeled garlic, cranberries, most of the herb leaves, 1½ tablespoons of red wine vinegar and 3 tablespoons of extra virgin olive oil to a coarse paste in a food processor, then season to perfection. Roughly chop the aubergine and courgettes, then toss all the veg with the dressing on a nice big serving platter.

4. Dice most of the halloumi into 2cm chunks, reserving a little, and slice the chillies 2cm thick, then skewer it all up – I like to use little rosemary skewers for bonus flavour. Preheat a large shallow cast-iron pan on the grill. Spritz with olive oil and pour in 2 ladles' worth of batter – it will spread out like a thin pancake. After 1 minute, spritz it with oil and finely grate over a little lemon zest and reserved halloumi. Cook for 4 minutes, then flip for just 2 minutes on the other side. Remove and repeat with the remaining batter. Grill the halloumi skewers on the bars alongside, turning until golden.

5. To serve, dollop the yoghurt over the dressed veg, then, holding the pomegranate half cut side down in the palm of your hand, bash the back with a spoon so all the seeds tumble out over the top. Pick over the remaining herbs and any reserved fennel tops, add the halloumi skewers and serve with the pancakes for tearing and scooping!

Grilled chilli & lemon chicken

Serves 6 | Prep 30 minutes | Cook 1 hour, plus resting

9 mixed-colour chillies

1 long red pepper

1 bulb of garlic

4 bay leaves

½ teaspoon dried red chilli flakes

1 bunch of thyme (20g)

1 lemon

1 x 1.5kg whole chicken

optional: sprigs of bay, thyme and rosemary

Bringing piri piri vibes, here we're making an incredible sauce to use as both a marinade for cooking and a salsa to serve, meaning double flavour impact.

1 Light the barbecue (pages 16–19). Prick the chillies and pepper and, as the barbecue heats up, char the chillies, pepper and whole garlic bulb over the hot zone, lid on, vents open.

2 Use tongs to toast the bay leaves on the grill for 30 seconds, then tear into a pestle and mortar, discarding the stalks. Add the chilli flakes and a pinch of sea salt, strip in the thyme and pound well. Use a speed peeler to strip in the lemon peel and pound again into a rough paste (you can use a small food processor for this step, if you prefer). Remove the thick white pith from the lemon, then finely chop the flesh. Muddle into the pestle and mortar with 2 tablespoons each of red wine vinegar and extra virgin olive oil.

3 Scrape away the larger bits of charred skin from the chillies and pepper, discarding the seeds and stalks, peel the garlic, then finely chop it all. Scrape into the pestle and mortar, mix together and season to perfection.

4 Use a large sharp knife to carefully cut down the back of the chicken, so you can open it out flat like a book, then score the legs. Reserve half the sauce in a small bowl for serving, then rub the rest over the chicken, getting into all the nooks and crannies. Place on the cool zone, skin side up, tucking extra woody herb sprigs around the edge to protect the chicken as it cooks, if you like, and cook lid on, vents open, for 1 hour, or until juicy and cooked through and the internal temperature is 65–70°C. Move to a clean board to rest for 30 minutes (the internal temp needs to reach 75°C).

5 Spoon over the remaining sauce and clank up the chicken. Great with Grilled chips (page 222) or sweet potato wedges, or my Sriracha corn (page 94).

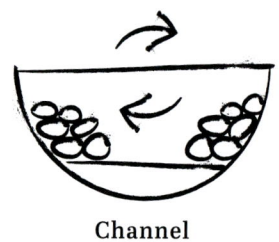

Channel

Herby leg of lamb & creamy beans

Serves 10 | Prep 25 minutes | Cook 1 hour, plus resting

4 leeks

1 bunch of mixed soft herbs (30g), such as mint, tarragon, basil, parsley

2 cloves of garlic

50g shelled unsalted pistachio nuts

2 lemons

100g breadcrumbs

2.2kg butterflied leg of lamb, bone out (ask your butcher to do this for you)

2 tablespoons Dijon mustard

1 bunch of sage (20g)

200g ripe cherry tomatoes

2 x 570g jars of cannellini beans

1 Soak a handful of wood chips in water according to the packet instructions. Light the barbecue (pages 16–19). Blacken the leeks directly on the coals for 10 to 15 minutes, turning halfway, then remove to a board.

2 Meanwhile, pick the soft herb leaves into a pestle and mortar with a pinch of sea salt, pound into a coarse paste, then peel and pound in the garlic. Roughly pound in the pistachios, then muddle in 2 tablespoons of extra virgin olive oil, squeeze in the juice of 1 lemon and scrunch in the breadcrumbs until combined (blitz in a food processor, if you prefer).

3 Lay the lamb out like an open book and massage all over with salt, black pepper and 1 tablespoon of olive oil. Sear on the hot zone for 5 minutes, or until gnarly, turning regularly with tongs, then move to a board, skin side down. Massage the top with the mustard, then pat on the herby crumbs.

4 Peel off and discard the outer charred layers of the leeks, cut into 2cm lengths and place in a 20cm x 25cm roasting tray. Rub half the sage leaves with olive oil, then add to the tray with the tomatoes and a generous splash of water. Carefully remove the grill and place the tray directly in the cool zone. Replace the grill, then sit the lamb, crumb side up, on the bars over the tray. Halve the remaining lemon and tuck it under the side of the lamb nearest the coals. Drain the wood chips and place on the hot zone with the remaining sage sprigs. Cook lid on, top vent half open above the meat for 30 minutes.

5 Carefully lift up the lamb and the grill and pour the beans into the tray, juice and all. Replace the grill and lamb and cook for a further 10 to 15 minutes with the lid on, top vent half open, or until the internal temperature reaches 55°C. Remove the lamb to rest, covered, for 30 minutes (the internal temp should rise to 60°C), leaving the beans to reduce for another 15 minutes.

6 Mix 1 tablespoon of red wine vinegar into the beans, season to perfection, then slice and add the lamb. Great with crusty bread and a green salad.

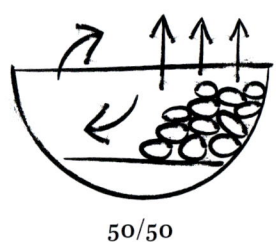

50/50

Pulled beef tacos

Serves 10 | Prep 30 minutes | Cook 3 hours

4 cloves

2 bay leaves

2 teaspoons English mustard

1.2kg shin of beef, bone in

3 red onions

2 large carrots

10 rashers of smoked streaky bacon

1 bunch of mixed woody herbs (20g), such as sage, rosemary

1 heaped teaspoon orange marmalade

150ml Worcestershire sauce

4 pickled walnuts

2 eating apples

250g white cabbage

80g watercress

4 limes

10 mini flour tortillas

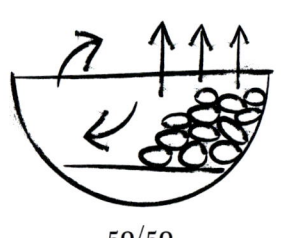

50/50

1 Light the barbecue (pages 16–19). Put 1 teaspoon of sea salt and 2 teaspoons of black pepper into a pestle and mortar with the cloves and bay (stalks removed) and pound well, then muddle in the mustard and 2 tablespoons of olive oil to make a paste. Rub it all over the beef, then place on the hot zone for 25 minutes, turning with tongs to build up a nice crust, and moving it from the hot to the medium zone as needed to control how quickly it colours.

2 Peel, halve and add 2 onions to the grill, turning with tongs until nicely bar-marked, then move to a board and chop into rough 1cm chunks. Chop the carrots a similar size. Slice the bacon and put in a large deep cast-iron pan on the hot zone with 1 tablespoon of olive oil. Strip in the herb leaves and cook until golden, stirring occasionally.

3 Add the chopped onions and carrots and cook for 10 minutes, stirring regularly, then stir in the marmalade and Worcestershire sauce. Finely slice and add the walnuts, then use tongs to move the beef into the pan and carefully move to the cool zone. Put the lid on the pan, and the barbecue lid on, top vent half open. Cook for 2 hours 30 minutes, or until the meat easily pulls apart. Halfway through, add a splash of water to the pan and baste the meat. The barbecue temperature should sit at around 180°C throughout.

4 Matchstick the apples, use a sharp knife or a speed peeler to finely shred the cabbage, peel and finely chop the remaining onion. Pile on a plate with the watercress, squeeze over the juice of 2 limes and add a pinch of salt.

5 Use tongs to – one by one – wipe the tortillas through the fat on the surface of the pan, then place on the cool zone of the grill. Use two forks to pull the meat apart, then shake the marrow out of the bone and mix through. Season to perfection, then serve it all at the table with the pot of English mustard and the remaining lime wedges, and let everyone build their own.

Pomegranate & harissa chicken

Serves 6 | Prep 10 minutes, plus marinating | Cook 1 hour 10 minutes, plus resting

1 onion

2 cloves of garlic

1 pomegranate

2 tablespoons rose harissa

3 tablespoons runny honey

1 x 1.5kg whole chicken

1 lemon

optional: 1 bunch of woody herbs (20g)

1. Peel and roughly chop the onion and garlic and place it all in a blender. Halve the pomegranate and, holding one half cut side down in the palm of your hand, bash the back with a spoon so all the seeds tumble out into the blender, reserving the other half. Add the harissa, honey, 2 tablespoons of olive oil and a pinch of sea salt and black pepper, and blitz until smooth.

2. Reserving a quarter of the sauce, rub the rest over the chicken really well. Leave to marinate for 30 minutes. Light the barbecue (pages 16–19).

3. Place the chicken, breast side down, over the cool zone, so the breasts are in the middle and the legs are closer to the hot zone on either side. Cook with the lid on, top vent half open, for 1 hour 10 minutes, or until golden and cooked through (the internal temperature should be 65–70°C), turning breast side up halfway through. When you turn it, halve and add the lemon, and baste the chicken with olive oil using the herbs as a brush, if you like.

4. Spread the reserved sauce across a serving platter, sit the chicken on top and let it rest for 30 minutes – the internal temp needs to reach 75°C.

5. Holding the remaining pomegranate half cut side down in the palm of your hand, bash the back with a spoon so all the seeds tumble out over the chicken, then squeeze over the charred lemon juice. Great served with Crispy chickpea houmous (page 214) or Squash, sage & rice salad (page 102).

Rôtisserie it up! If you have a clockwork rôtisserie kit and the means to build a firepit, I'd recommend it! Set up hot and medium zones and get the rôtisserie ready in line with the medium part. Carefully thread the chicken on to the rôtisserie skewer, with a lemon half at each end. Set it into the rôtisserie about 40cm from the medium coals (and no higher than 60cm). Cook as above, keeping the fire as even as possible.

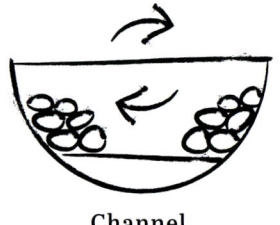

Channel

Ultimate pork ribs 3 ways

Serves 6–8 | 2 hours 30 minutes, plus resting

1.4kg baby back ribs

⅓ x Bay salt (page 218)

50g unsalted butter

50ml cider

½ an orange

Choose your glaze:
BBQ sauce

½ x Store-cupboard BBQ sauce (page 202)

Hoisin

200ml hoisin sauce

1 orange

Mango chutney

½ a pomegranate

1 jar of mango chutney

1. Light the barbecue (pages 16–19). Soak a handful of wood chips according to the packet instructions. Rub the Bay salt (page 218) all over the ribs and place on the cool zone. Drain the wood chips and place them on the hot zone. Cook with the lid on, top vent half open, for 1 hour, or until golden, turning halfway.

2. Lay out a double layer of thick tin foil (30cm long) and top with a large sheet of greaseproof paper. Place 1 rack of ribs in the centre of the sheet, dot with butter, drizzle with cider, then sit the other rack(s) on top and repeat. Slice and lay over the orange. Fold in the foil overhang, tightly rolling in the sides to seal. Return to the cool zone and cook lid on, top vent half open, for 1 hour.

3. Meanwhile, make your chosen glaze. Whip up a batch of Store-cupboard BBQ sauce (page 202), mix the hoisin with the orange juice until smooth, or squeeze the pomegranate juice into a bowl and mix with the mango chutney.

4. Unwrap the ribs and check the meat is soft and tender, then carefully pour any cooking juices into your glaze. Transfer the ribs to the medium-hot zone and use a pastry brush or the back of a spoon to glaze them all over. Cook with the lid on, top vent open, for 5 to 10 minutes, or until the glaze sets, basting occasionally (at this stage the temperature will be low, so if you've got guests coming round it will hold the ribs beautifully until you're ready to dish up!).

5. Serve the ribs on a big board or platter with garnishes of your choice or like you see in the picture, slice up and dig in!

Ingredient know-how: You can ask your butcher to remove the membrane on the underside of the ribs – I personally like it though, for a bit of added flavour and texture.

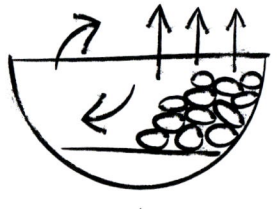

50/50

Buddy's chicken Caesar

Serves 6–8 | **1 hour 30 minutes, plus resting**

- 1 bunch of mixed woody herbs (20g)
- 1 x 2kg whole chicken
- 3 lemons
- 4 x 3cm-thick slices of sourdough bread
- 1 sweetheart cabbage
- 4 mixed-colour chillies
- 1 x 50g tin of anchovy fillets
- ½ teaspoon dried oregano
- 1 clove of garlic
- 1 heaped teaspoon English mustard
- 2 tablespoons Worcestershire sauce
- 4 heaped tablespoons Greek yoghurt
- 60g Parmesan cheese
- 200g tenderstem broccoli
- 12 rashers of smoked streaky bacon
- 2 romaine lettuces

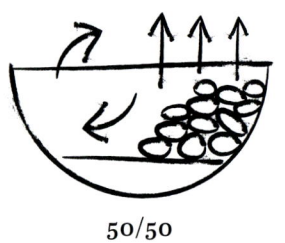

50/50

1. Light the barbecue (pages 16–19). Soak a handful of wood chips according to the packet instructions. Strip half the herb leaves into a pestle and mortar, pound with a pinch of sea salt and black pepper, then muddle in 2 tablespoons of olive oil. Use a large sharp knife to carefully cut down the back of the chicken, so you can open it out flat. Rub it all over with the herby oil, then place skin side down on the hot zone to sear for 5 minutes, flipping halfway. Halve and char 2 lemons alongside. Put the bread on the cool zone.

2. Drain the wood chips and place on the hot zone with half the remaining herb sprigs for bonus fragrance. Move the chicken on top of the bread with the legs towards the medium zone and scatter over the last of the herbs. Place the cabbage on the hot zone. Prick the chillies and place on the medium-cool zone. Cook lid on, top vent half open, for 1 hour, or until the chicken internal temperature is 65–70°C, spritzing with oil occasionally, and removing the lemons and chillies after 20 minutes.

3. Once cool enough to handle, scrape the blackened skin off the chillies, discard the seeds and stalks, then slice lengthways and lay on a plate with the anchovies. Squeeze over half the fresh lemon juice, sprinkle over the dried oregano, add a few drips of extra virgin olive oil, and set aside.

4. For the dressing, bash the garlic into a paste in a pestle and mortar. Mix in the mustard, Worcestershire sauce and yoghurt. Finely grate in the Parmesan, squeeze in 3 of the charred lemon halves, then finely chop and add one of them, along with a drizzle of oil from the anchovy tin. Season to perfection.

5. Remove the chicken and bread to a board and rest the chicken for 30 minutes – the internal temp needs to reach 75°C. Trim the broccoli, halving any thicker stalks lengthways. Lay the bacon on the hot zone, scatter over the broccoli and cook lid on, top vent half open, for 10 to 15 minutes, removing once golden.

6. Tear up the toasts. Click apart the lettuce leaves. Trim the cabbage, remove the outer burnt layers and roughly slice. Toss it all through the dressing with the bacon and broccoli. Serve with the golden chicken and anchovies.

Veggie gumbo

Serves 6–8 | **1 hour 10 minutes**

3 heaped tablespoons plain flour

1 onion

4 green peppers

4 jalapeño chillies

2 cloves of garlic

3 sticks of celery

2 corn on the cob

200g okra

4 spring onions

2 tablespoons Old Bay seasoning

1 x 570g jar of chickpeas

1 x 400g tin of plum tomatoes

1 litre veg stock

4 sprigs of flat-leaf parsley

I've been lucky enough to taste some truly incredible gumbos with the good people of New Orleans, and this veggie version is inspired by those epic dishes.

1. Light the barbecue (pages 16–19). Put 3 tablespoons of olive oil into a large shallow cast-iron casserole pan on the medium-hot zone and stir in the flour to make a paste. Cook until dark brown, stirring constantly. Meanwhile, halve the unpeeled onion, prick the peppers and jalapeños, then char on the hot zone with the unpeeled garlic, the celery, corn, okra and spring onions for 15 minutes, turning regularly and moving to the cool zone if colouring too quickly. Remove to your board once charred. You may need to work in batches.

2. Once cool enough to handle, peel and finely chop the onion and garlic, and add to the pan with the Old Bay. Cook for 5 minutes, or until softened and dark nutty brown, stirring regularly.

3. Scrape the blackened skin off the peppers, discard the seeds and stalks, then chop up with the celery and okra. Use a large sharp knife to cut the corn kernels off the cobs and add it all to the pan with the chickpeas, juice and all. Tip in the tomatoes, breaking them up with your spoon, pour in the stock, then carefully move the pan to the cool zone. Cook with the lid on, vents open, for 45 minutes, or until the veg is tender and the stew is gloriously thick.

4. Meanwhile, trim and roughly chop the charred spring onions and jalapeños, discarding the stalks, then mix with 1 tablespoon of red wine vinegar and a pinch of sea salt, and set aside to quickly pickle.

5. Season the stew to perfection, spoon over the pickled veg, pick over the parsley leaves and serve. Great with a pan of hot fluffy rice.

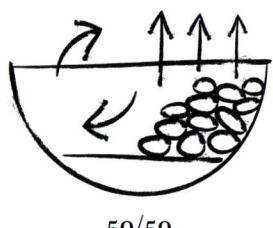

50/50

Fruity pork chops & grilled potatoes

Serves 6–8 | 1 hour

1kg new potatoes

1 bunch of spring onions

800g stone fruit, such as plums, peaches, apricots

1 bunch of sage (20g)

4 cloves of garlic

2 bay leaves

150ml whisky

1 tablespoon runny honey

4 x 400g thick pork chops, bone in, skin removed

1. Light the barbecue (pages 16–19). Wash the potatoes, slice 1cm thick and put aside. Trim and halve the spring onions. Halve and destone the fruit. Grill the spring onions and fruit on the hot-medium zone until bar-marked, turning regularly with tongs and moving to the cool zone if colouring too quickly.

2. Put a large shallow cast-iron casserole pan on the cool zone with 1 tablespoon of olive oil. Pick in the sage leaves and, once starting to crisp up, add the grilled spring onions. Peel, slice and add the garlic, along with the bay. Move the stone fruit into the pan as it's done.

3. Pour in the whisky and carefully flame it, if you like (stand back!), then add the honey and a pinch of sea salt and black pepper. Carefully move the pan to the hot zone and let it all reduce for 10 minutes, or until soft, sticky and the fruit has started to break down, adding splashes of water to keep it syrupy. Remove the pan to a heatproof surface.

4. Score into the fat on the pork chops at 1cm intervals, ½cm deep. Season with salt, spritz with olive oil, then grill for 5 to 10 minutes on the hot or medium zone, turning halfway and moving to the cooler zone if your coals flare up. Sit the chops in the pan and carefully move it back to the cool zone so the chops can cook through for 5 more minutes. Remove, cover and leave to rest.

5. Use tongs to lay the potato slices on the hot zone, and cook with the lid on, vents open, for 5 minutes, or until bar-marked, then move to the medium-cool zone, lid on, vents open, for another 10 to 15 minutes, or until cooked through, turning regularly and spritzing with oil. Dish it all up together, slicing the pork to serve. Great with a simple green salad.

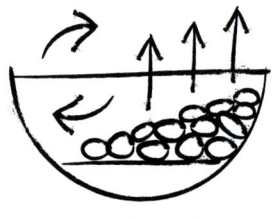

Graduated

Super surf & turf mixed grill

Serves 4 | 45 minutes

2 spring onions

2 cloves of garlic

2 lemons

1 teaspoon baby capers in brine

1 x 50g tin of anchovy fillets

½ a bunch of mixed soft herbs (15g)

250g soft unsalted butter

½ a bulb of fennel

160g green beans

½ a sourdough or French baguette

4 chicken thighs, skin on, bone in

100g chorizo

8 raw shell-on king prawns

600g mixed mussels & clams, scrubbed, debearded

160g ripe cherry tomatoes

60ml white wine

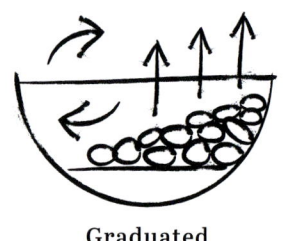

Graduated

1. To make a flavoured butter, trim and roughly chop the spring onions, peel the garlic and finely grate the zest of 1 lemon, then blitz it all in a food processor with the capers, anchovies and most of the soft herb leaves (or chop by hand on a board). Blitz or mix in the soft butter until combined.

2. Trim the fennel and cut into thin wedges, trim the green beans and slice the baguette at an angle. Rub the chicken with 2 tablespoons of olive oil and season with sea salt and black pepper. Slice the chorizo 1cm thick. Peel the prawns, leaving the heads and tails on, then run a small sharp knife down the back of each, discarding the vein. Check the mussels and clams, tap any open ones and if they don't close, discard. Light the barbecue (pages 16–19).

3. Place the chicken skin side down in a large shallow cast-iron pan on the hot zone, then add the chorizo and cook lid on, vents open, for 10 minutes, or until the fat has rendered out and the skin is crisp. Flip the chicken over and place it directly on the medium zone to cook lid on, vents open, for 10 minutes, or until cooked through (the internal temperature should be 75°C), turning regularly, then move to a serving platter with the chorizo.

4. Cook the fennel in the rendered fat in the pan for 5 minutes, then add the green beans for 2 more minutes, turning until golden. Transfer the beans to the platter, and the fennel to the cool zone. Cook the tomatoes in the pan for 2 minutes, or until blistered. Toast the bread in the pan at the same time, turning and spritzing with olive oil, as needed, then arrange it all on the platter.

5. Tip the mussels, clams and prawns into the pan. Pour in the wine and add 3 tablespoons of flavoured butter. Cook lid on, vents open, for 5 minutes, or until the clams and mussels have opened (discard any that remain closed) and the prawns are cooked through, then transfer to the platter with the fennel. Spoon over the lovely hot pan juices, pick over the remaining herbs, and serve with lemon wedges. The leftover flavoured butter will keep for up to 2 weeks in the fridge, or up to 3 months in the freezer. Fast future flavour awaits!

Duck legs & plum sauce

Serves 4 | **Prep 10 minutes** | **Cook 2 hours**

4 teaspoons Bay salt (page 218)

4 duck legs

8 plums

1 bunch of woody herbs (20g), such as bay, thyme, oregano, rosemary

1 sweetheart cabbage

300g wholegrain basmati rice

6 bay leaves

1 x 570g jar of chickpeas

4 tablespoons Greek yoghurt

1. Light the barbecue (pages 16–19). Place a roasting tray with 400ml of water underneath the grill in the cool zone – this will help the duck legs steam and you'll capture lovely juices.

2. Rub the Bay salt (page 218) all over the duck legs, then place them on the hot zone for 5 minutes, or until golden all over, turning regularly. Move to the cool zone over the tray and cook with the lid on, vents open, for 1 hour.

3. When the time's up, line up the plums next to the duck on the cool zone. Place the bunch of herbs on the hot zone, sit the cabbage on top, and cook it all with the lid on, vents open, for a further 1 hour, or until the duck meat pulls away from the bone, topping up the tray with more water if it looks dry (don't be alarmed when the cabbage and herbs blacken – they're meant to!).

4. With 35 minutes to go, place the rice, bay and a small pinch of sea salt in a cast-iron pan with 500ml of boiling kettle water and the chickpeas, juice and all. Place on the medium zone to cook lid on, vents open for 30 minutes, then carefully remove the pan from the grill, cover and steam for 5 minutes.

5. Mash the plums in a shallow serving bowl, discarding the stones, then sit the duck legs on top. Trim the cabbage, removing the burnt outer layers, then thickly slice. Mix up the rice and chickpeas, season to perfection, and dish it all up together, rippling the plum sauce with the yoghurt, to serve.

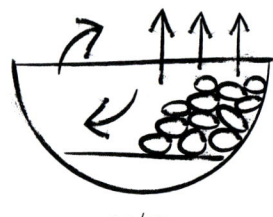

50/50

Veg-tastic barbecue mezze

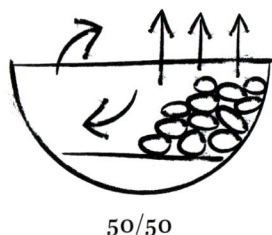

50/50

Mighty veg do wonderful things when grilled, blackened, charred and blistered – there are so many ways to create big flavour. I'm sharing a few of my favourites here, and the recipes on these pages make a spectacular spread when all cooked together. Plus, I've added a couple of supplementary dishes that really finish off the party – namely a beautiful labneh, easy sesame flatbread and a flavour-boosted tin of anchovies. Feel free to pick and choose the elements that make your heart sing, or go all out and cook everything up for a veg-tastic feast.

Mint & chilli courgettes

Serves 6 | 25 minutes

Light the barbecue (pages 16–19). Place **2 courgettes** on the hot zone and cook lid on, vents open, for 20 minutes, or until charred, turning occasionally. Roughly chop, scrape into a bowl, then chop and add the leaves from **a few sprigs of mint**. Finely slice and add **1 fresh red chilli**, then mix with ½ a tablespoon of red wine vinegar and 1 tablespoon of extra virgin olive oil and season to perfection.

Burnt butter labneh

Serves 6 | 10 minutes, plus draining

Light the barbecue (pages 16–19). Place a sieve over a bowl and line with a few sheets of kitchen paper. Tip in **500g of Greek yoghurt**, add a pinch of sea salt, then pull up the paper around the yoghurt and very gently apply pressure so that the liquid starts to drip through into the bowl. Leave in the fridge to drain, until it becomes the consistency of cream cheese. Gently squeeze out and discard any remaining liquid, then tip the yoghurt into a serving bowl. Finely grate in the zest of **1 lemon**, squeeze in the juice and mix to make labneh. Melt **50g of unsalted butter** in a cast-iron pan on the medium zone until browned (or in a pan over a medium heat on the hob), then stir in **2 tablespoons of dukkah** and pour over the labneh. Nice with a few **thyme tips**, if you have them.

Anchovies & orange

Serves 6 | 3 minutes

Take **1 x 50g tin of anchovy fillets in oil**, squeeze over the juice from **½ an orange**, then finely chop and add **a few soft herbs, like parsley or mint leaves, or leafy fennel tops**.

Halloumi & apricots

Serves 6 | 25 minutes

Light the barbecue (pages 16–19). Pat dry, then lightly score a **225g block of halloumi**, drizzle with 1 tablespoon of olive oil and cook on the hot zone for 10 minutes, or until soft, golden and bar-marked, turning halfway. Cook **6 ripe apricots** alongside until beautifully charred, turning occasionally, then, once cool enough to handle, tear into an ovenproof dish, discarding the stones. Sit the halloumi on top, then pick over a few **thyme leaves**. Drizzle with 1 tablespoon of oil and **1 teaspoon of runny honey**, if you like, and return to the cool zone for a few extra minutes, or until bubbling.

Baba ganoush

Serves 6 | 25 minutes

Light the barbecue (pages 16–19). Prick **2 aubergines (250g each)**, place on the hot zone and cook lid on, vents open, for 20 minutes, or until soft and blackened, turning occasionally, then remove (or cook the aubergines directly on the coals, if you prefer). Slice them open and scoop the flesh into a bowl. Add **2 tablespoons of tahini** and the juice of **1 lemon**, finely grate in **½ a clove of garlic**, trim, finely slice and add **2 spring onions**, then finely chop and add **½ a bunch of flat-leaf parsley (15g)**, stalks and all. Roughly mash, season to perfection, and finish with a drizzle of extra virgin olive oil.

Sweet peppers & capers

Serves 6 | 25 minutes

Light the barbecue (pages 16–19). Prick **2 mixed-colour peppers**, place on the hot zone and cook lid on, vents open, for 20 minutes, or until blackened, turning occasionally and adding **6 pricked padrón peppers** for the final 5 minutes. Once cool enough to handle, remove the skins from just the mixed-colour peppers, then finely slice all the peppers into long strips and place in a bowl, discarding the seeds and stalks. Destone and tear over **5 olives**, then scrunch over **1 tablespoon of baby capers in brine** and add a little red wine vinegar. Use a speed peeler to remove the peel of **½ a lemon**, slice into very thin strips and scatter over, then finish with a drizzle of extra virgin olive oil, if you like.

Tear & share flatbread

Serves 6 | 8 minutes, plus resting

You need an even heat to cook this bread, so carefully shake out your hot coals to evenly cover the base of the barbecue. In a bowl, mix **300g of self-raising flour** with a pinch of sea salt, **250g of natural yoghurt** and 2 tablespoons of olive oil until you have a dough, then cover and leave to rest for at least 15 minutes. Sprinkle **2 tablespoons of sesame seeds** over the dough and roll out on a flour-dusted surface into one large flatbread that's just under ½cm thick. Use the rolling pin to gently roll it up, then unroll it on to the grill and cook for 3 minutes, or until golden, turning halfway.

Paprika pulled pork

Serves 10 | 2 hours 15 minutes, plus resting

2kg piece of skinless, boneless pork shoulder

1 tablespoon smoked paprika

1 Light the barbecue (pages 16–19) and soak a handful of wood chips according to the packet instructions, if you like. Place a roasting tray with 400ml of water underneath the grill in the cool zone – this will help the pork steam and you'll capture lovely juices.

2 Cut the pork into 4 equal chunks, drizzle with 1 tablespoon each of red wine vinegar and olive oil, then rub all over with the paprika and a big pinch of sea salt and black pepper. Sear on the hot zone for 10 minutes, turning regularly and moving to the medium or cool zone if colouring too quickly.

3 Once seared, move the pork chunks to the cool zone above the tray of water and cook with the lid on, top vent half open, for 2 hours, or until the pork is gnarly and pullable with a dark bark, turning occasionally. Rest the pork for 30 minutes, loosely covered with tin foil.

4 Carefully skim away most of the fat from the tray. Shred and pull apart the meat with two forks, discarding any gristly bits, then toss with the tasty juices in the tray. Great served with a simple slaw and a stack of soft brioche buns (or make your own buns, page 224), as well as English mustard, or your favourite condiments like Store-cupboard BBQ sauce (page 202), Chilli sauce (page 204), or my Smoky ketchup (page 212).

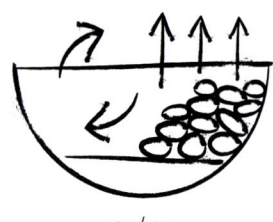

50/50

Burgers & patties

Gravy cheeseburgers

Serves 4 | 25 minutes

500g beef mince (20% fat)

¼ of a cucumber

1 large ripe tomato

1 red onion

½ teaspoon creamed horseradish

½ a bunch of flat-leaf parsley (15g)

2 rashers of smoked streaky bacon

1 teaspoon Marmite

2 tablespoons plain flour

500ml beef stock

2 teaspoons English mustard

4 heaped tablespoons mayo (or make your own, page 210)

40g Cheddar cheese

4 burger buns (or make your own, page 224)

1. Scrunch the mince well, then divide equally into four and shape into patties just under 1cm thick. Season well with sea salt and black pepper.

2. Slice the cucumber at an angle. Slice the tomato ½cm thick. Peel and very finely slice most of the red onion into rounds, reserving a third. Place it all in a bowl, season with salt, add 1 tablespoon of red wine vinegar and the horseradish, then scrunch together well. Drizzle with 1 tablespoon of extra virgin olive oil, and pick over the parsley.

3. Finely chop the reserved onion third, finely slice the bacon, then cook in a frying pan over a medium-high heat on the hob with a drizzle of olive oil for 5 minutes, or until the onion is softened and the bacon is golden. Stir in the Marmite, then the flour for 1 minute. Gradually stir in the stock, simmer for a few minutes, or until thickened, then season to perfection with black pepper.

4. Mix the mustard into the mayo. Slice the cheese. Halve the buns. Light the barbecue (pages 16–19). Cook the burgers on the hot zone for 3 to 4 minutes on each side, moving to the medium zone if they're colouring too quickly, then lay over the cheese, put the lid on, vents open, and let the cheese melt for a minute, toasting the buns alongside. Reheat the gravy, if needed.

5. In the buns, layer up the mustard mayo, quick-pickled veg and burgers in whatever way makes you happy, squash together, dunk in the gravy, and devour! Serve the extra pickled veg on the side.

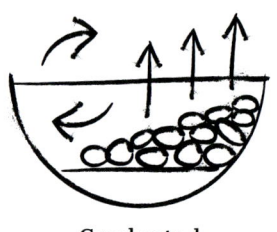

Graduated

Miso mushroom burgers

Serves 4 | 25 minutes

- 2 tablespoons miso
- 2 tablespoons mirin
- 1 tablespoon low-salt soy sauce
- 1 tablespoon maple syrup
- 1 large ripe avocado
- 2 limes
- 160g white cabbage
- ½ a cucumber (160g)
- 4 large portobello mushrooms
- 1 bunch of spring onions
- 4 burger buns (or make your own, page 224)

1 To make the glaze, mix the miso with 1 tablespoon of mirin, the soy and maple until combined. Halve and destone the avo, scoop the flesh into a bowl, mash with the remaining mirin and the juice of ½ a lime, and season to perfection. Use a speed peeler to finely shred the cabbage, then dress with the juice of 1 lime and a pinch of sea salt and black pepper. Use a speed peeler to peel the cucumber into ribbons. Light the barbecue (pages 16–19).

2 Trim the mushroom stalks, then grill the mushrooms on the hot zone, lid on, vents open, for 2 minutes, turning halfway. Move them to the cool zone and cook for a further 6 minutes, turning every minute and brushing with the glaze on each turn. Char the spring onions alongside, then remove to your board, trim, chop and mix with the cabbage. Halve and toast the buns.

3 Spread the bun bases with avo, layer up with some cabbage and spring onions, the mushrooms and some cucumber ribbons, spread any leftover glaze on the bun tops, then squash together, serving excess veg on the side.

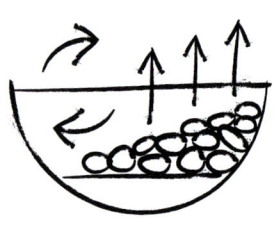

Graduated

Lamb moussaka burgers

Serves 4 | 30 minutes

200g feta cheese

500g lamb mince (20% fat)

½ teaspoon ground cumin

4 burger buns (or make your own, page 224)

1 aubergine (250g)

320g ripe tomatoes on the vine

4 spring onions

1 bunch of flat-leaf parsley (30g)

1. Blitz the feta in a small blender or food processor with 120ml of water until smooth, loosening with extra splashes of water, if needed, until drizzleable. Pour half into a bowl, stashing the rest in the fridge, where it will keep happily for up to 3 days. Light the barbecue (pages 16–19).

2. Scrunch the mince well, then divide equally into four and shape into 1cm-thick patties. Sprinkle the cumin on a plate with a pinch of sea salt and black pepper, then turn the burgers in the seasoning to coat. Halve the buns.

3. Slice the aubergine lengthways 1cm thick. Place on the hot zone with the vine of tomatoes and the whole spring onions, turning regularly, and removing to a board when soft and charred. Trim the spring onions, then finely chop with the aubergine and tomatoes, discarding the tomato vine. Mix with 1 tablespoon of red wine vinegar and season to perfection. Pick the parsley leaves and dress with a little extra virgin olive oil.

4. Cook the lamb burgers on the hot zone for 2 minutes on each side, or until cooked through, moving to the medium zone if they're colouring too quickly, and toasting the buns alongside.

5. Layer up the moussaka veg mixture, the burgers and blitzed feta, pile the dressed parsley on top, put the lids on, and enjoy!

Leftover love: Leftover blitzed feta is delicious drizzled over grilled veg, salad or eggs, or used to dress beans or chickpeas.

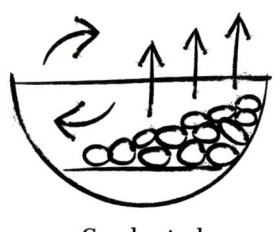

Graduated

Sesame chicken burgers

Serves 4 | 30 minutes

1 lime

1 tablespoon gochujang paste

4 tablespoons Greek yoghurt, plus extra to serve

1 red pepper

4 spring onions

160g white cabbage

½ a cucumber (160g)

2 sprigs of mint

4 burger buns (or make your own, page 224)

2 tablespoons sesame seeds

500g chicken mince (20% fat)

1 Light the barbecue (pages 16–19). Finely grate and reserve the lime zest. In a little bowl, mix the gochujang and yoghurt with a squeeze of lime juice until smooth, then season with sea salt. Deseed and very finely slice the red pepper, trim and finely slice the spring onions, very finely shred the cabbage, scratch the outside of the cucumber with a fork to create grooves, then finely slice into rounds. Finely slice the mint leaves. Dress it all with the remaining lime juice and 1 tablespoon of extra virgin olive oil, scrunch well, and season to perfection. Halve the buns.

2 Put the sesame seeds on a small plate. Season the mince well with salt and black pepper, then scrunch with the lime zest. Divide equally into four and shape into 2cm-thick patties, dipping into the sesame seeds to coat all over.

3 Spritz the burgers with olive oil and cook on the hot zone for 6 minutes on each side, or until golden and cooked through, moving to the medium zone if they're colouring too quickly, and toasting the buns alongside.

4 Layer up the gochujang yoghurt, quick pickled veg and burgers. Spoon over more yoghurt, and get the tops on, serving the remaining veg on the side.

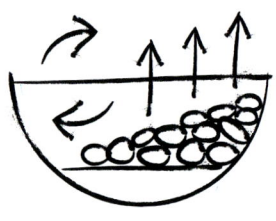

Graduated

Blue cheese pork burgers

Serves 4 | 20 minutes

½ a bunch of chives (10g)

8 cornichons

1 small eating apple

1 lemon

1 heaped teaspoon Dijon mustard

1 little gem lettuce

1 handful of lamb's lettuce

50g shelled walnut halves

500g pork mince

4 burger buns (or make your own, page 224)

100g Stilton cheese

3 tablespoons crème fraîche

1. For a delicate salsa, finely chop the chives and finely slice the cornichons. Very finely dice the apple. Squeeze over half the lemon juice, mix and set aside.

2. To make a French dressing, whisk the mustard, remaining lemon juice and 3 tablespoons of extra virgin olive oil in a bowl, then season to perfection with sea salt. Put 1 tablespoon of dressing aside, then click apart the gem and add to the bowl with the lamb's lettuce, ready to toss at the last minute.

3. For the patties, crush the walnuts, then mix into the mince with a pinch of salt and black pepper. Divide equally into four, shape into 1cm-thick patties and spritz with olive oil. Light the barbecue (pages 16–19).

4. Sear the burgers on the hot zone for 90 seconds on each side, then brush with the reserved French dressing and cook for a further 3 minutes on each side, or until golden and cooked through, brushing with more dressing when you turn them and moving to the medium zone if they're colouring too quickly. Toast the buns alongside. Crumble the Stilton into a small enamel tray, add the crème fraîche and melt on the cool zone, stirring occasionally, then remove.

5. Layer up the oozy cheese, dressed leaves, burgers and salsa in the buns. Serve with the extra dressed leaves and oozy cheese on the side, for dunking.

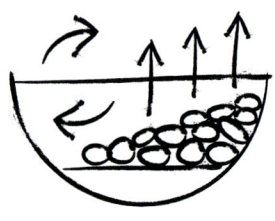

Graduated

Beet & feta bean burgers

Serves 4 | **25 minutes, plus chilling**

2 red onions

160g frozen broad beans

1 x 400g tin of chickpeas

1 x 250g packet of cooked mixed quinoa

1 heaped teaspoon ground cumin

1 heaped teaspoon smoked paprika

160g vac-packed beetroots

4 burger buns (or make your own, page 224)

½ a bunch of soft herbs (15g), such as mint, flat-leaf parsley

4 tablespoons natural yoghurt

50g feta cheese

1. Peel 1 onion, then quarter it and break into petals. Dry fry with the frozen broad beans in a large frying pan on a high heat on the hob for 5 minutes, or until charred and softened, tossing regularly, then tip it all into a food processor (of course, if you have the barbecue lit for other things, you could char it all in a metal sieve over the grill instead).

2. Drain the chickpeas and add to the processor with the quinoa, spices, 1 teaspoon of red wine vinegar and a pinch of sea salt and black pepper. Blitz until finely chopped and combined, stopping to scrape down the sides, as needed. Use clean, wet hands to divide and shape the mixture into 4 patties about 2 to 3cm thick. Rub with olive oil, then chill in the fridge until needed.

3. Peel and very finely slice the remaining onion, then, in a bowl, scrunch with 1 tablespoon of red wine vinegar and a pinch of salt, and set aside to quickly pickle. Light the barbecue (pages 16–19).

4. Cook the burgers on the hot zone for 5 minutes, or until nicely charred, turning halfway, then move to the medium-cool zone and cook for another 5 minutes with the lid on, vents open, or until cooked through. Pat the beets dry with kitchen paper and char alongside the burgers for the last 5 minutes, turning occasionally. Halve and toast the buns.

5. Remove and finely slice the beets. Pick the herbs. Spread the bun bases with the yoghurt, add the burgers, beets, pickled red onion, herb leaves and a crumbling of feta, then pop the tops on and enjoy!

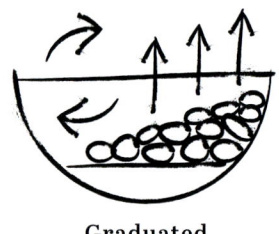

Graduated

Prawn toast burgers

Serves 4 as a main / 8 as a side | 20 minutes

1 cucumber (320g)

1 fresh red chilli

2 limes

2 tablespoons chilli jam

2 tablespoons Greek yoghurt

10cm piece of ginger

2 spring onions

500g raw peeled jumbo prawns

1 teaspoon English mustard

4 tablespoons mixed sesame seeds

4 burger buns (or make your own, page 224)

2 sprigs of coriander

1. Roughly peel the cucumber to make it stripy, then finely slice into rounds and place in a large bowl. Finely chop and add the chilli, then finely grate in the zest of 1 lime and squeeze in the juice. Toss together and season to perfection. Mix the chilli jam and yoghurt together.

2. Peel the ginger, trim the spring onions, then roughly chop and place in a food processor. Blitz until fairly fine, then pulse in the prawns, mustard and a pinch of sea salt and black pepper until just combined.

3. Put the sesame seeds on a small plate. Halve the buns. Divide the prawn mixture and spread over the eight bun halves, using the back of a spoon to spread to the edges. Light the barbecue (pages 16–19) and give the grill a really good brush to clean it – this will help prevent the burgers from sticking.

4. Dip the prawn side of each bun half into the sesame seeds, spritz with olive oil, then grill on the hot zone, sesame side down, for 5 minutes, or until cooked through, moving to the medium zone if they're colouring too quickly, and toasting the other side of each bun for just the last 30 seconds.

5. To serve, layer up the prawn toast bun halves with pickled cucumber and chilli yoghurt, then pick over the coriander leaves and serve with lime wedges.

Helpful hint: Try dividing the prawn mixture between baguette rounds for canape-sized toasts for lots of lucky people!

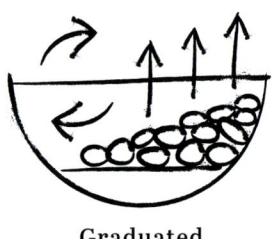

Graduated

Chorizo fish burgers

Serves 4 | 40 minutes

2 red peppers

25g blanched almonds

1 bunch of flat-leaf parsley (30g)

50g Manchego cheese

2 lemons

4 burger buns (or make your own, page 224)

75g chorizo

500g white fish fillets, skin off, pin-boned

1 egg

1 Light the barbecue (pages 16–19) and give the grill a really good brush to clean it – this will help prevent the burgers from sticking. Prick the peppers and char over the hot zone, lid on, vents open, for 10 minutes.

2 Meanwhile, in a pestle and mortar, pound the almonds until fine. Pound in half the parsley leaves (reserving the stalks) and finely grate in the cheese. Finely grate and reserve the lemon zest, then squeeze in the juice of 1 lemon and muddle in 2 tablespoons of extra virgin olive oil and a pinch of black pepper (do this in a food processor, if you prefer). Halve the buns.

3 Scrape away the larger bits of charred skin from the peppers, then cut them into strips, discarding the seeds and stalks. Dress with ½ a tablespoon of extra virgin olive oil and 1 teaspoon of red wine vinegar and set aside.

4 Finely slice the parsley stalks and finely chop the chorizo and half the fish, mixing it all with the reserved lemon zest as you go, until super-fine. Chop the rest of the fish into small chunks, then chop through the mix. Scrunch in the egg, squashing and bringing it together well with clean hands.

5 Use the remaining parsley leaves to make 4 piles on your board the same diameter as your buns. Divide the burger mixture equally into four and, with wet hands, shape into balls, then flatten into 3cm-thick patties on top of the piles of parsley, sticking the leaves to one side of each burger.

6 Cook the burgers, parsley side down, over the hot zone for 6 minutes, moving to the medium zone if they're colouring too quickly, then gently flip them over to cook for 2 minutes on the other side, or until cooked through. Finely slice and grill the remaining lemon, toasting the buns alongside.

7 Spread the almond paste across the toasted buns, layer up the burgers, peppers and grilled lemon slices, pop the tops on and enjoy!

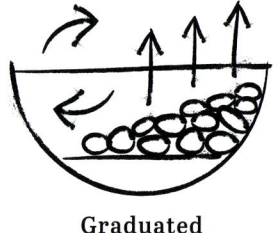

Graduated

Things that make the barbecue rock

Store-cupboard BBQ sauce

Makes 350ml | 20 minutes, plus cooling

1 cinnamon stick

2 bay leaves

1 lemon

1 clove of garlic

175g tomato ketchup

75g brown sauce

4 tablespoons Worcestershire sauce

2 tablespoons orange marmalade

1 teaspoon Marmite

2 teaspoons English mustard

2 tablespoons stem ginger syrup

50ml port or red wine

1 If you've got the barbecue going, use a cast-iron pan on the hot zone, or, if you're cooking inside, use a small pan over a high heat on the hob. Go in with 1 tablespoon of olive oil, the cinnamon stick and bay. Use a speed peeler to add a couple of strips of lemon peel, then squash and add the unpeeled garlic clove. Cook for 2 minutes, or until smelling fantastic, stirring regularly.

2 Stir in the ketchup, brown and Worcestershire sauces, marmalade, Marmite, mustard and stem ginger syrup. Pour in the port, bring to the boil, then cover (lid on, vents open, if using the barbecue), and simmer for about 10 minutes, or until thick, stirring occasionally. Pick out the cinnamon, bay, lemon peel and garlic, or pass through a coarse sieve, then season to perfection, if needed.

3 Leave to cool completely, then use right away, or store in the fridge in sterilized jars or bottles for up to 6 weeks. Once opened, use within 1 week. Great with my Ultimate pork ribs (page 158), Grilled chips (page 222) or Ultimate barbecue brekkie (pages 118–123).

Batch it up: This is a great recipe to double up so you have a good fridge stash, or to give away as gifts!

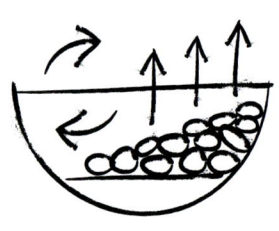

Graduated

Chilli sauce

Makes 550ml | 45 minutes, plus cooling

4 cloves of garlic

2 red peppers

10 fresh red chillies

2 teaspoons chilli powder

500g ripe tomatoes

150ml cider vinegar

3 tablespoons runny honey

250ml unsweetened apple juice

You can buy some incredible chilli sauces these days, and I have a whole range at home for different purposes. But when you have the time, you can't beat a batch of this homemade beauty! Double up, and make a friend happy, too.

1 Peel the garlic, deseed the peppers and chillies, roughly chop and cook it all in a large shallow casserole pan over a medium heat on the hob with 2 tablespoons of olive oil for 10 minutes, or until softened, stirring regularly.

2 Stir in the chilli powder, roughly chop and add the tomatoes, then the vinegar, honey, apple juice and 100ml of water. Simmer for 30 minutes, or until reduced by half, stirring occasionally. Carefully transfer the mixture into a blender, add 2 level teaspoons of sea salt and a pinch of black pepper, and blitz until smooth. You can leave the sauce as is, or you can pour it through a sieve to achieve a super-silky consistency. Either way, give it a taste, season to perfection, if needed, then cover and leave to cool completely.

3 Store in sterilized jars or bottles in a cool, dark place for up to 6 weeks. Once opened, keep in the fridge and use within 3 days. Great with my Chicken shawarma (page 56), or Halloumi fritters (page 130).

Flavour boost: Deseeding the chillies gives a medium heat, but feel free to leave the seeds in and go hotter, if you dare!

Salsa verde

Serves 8 | 10 minutes

½ a clove of garlic

1 x 50g tin of anchovy fillets in oil

1 tablespoon baby capers in brine

5 cornichons

1 tablespoon Dijon mustard

1 bunch of flat-leaf parsley (30g)

½ a bunch of basil (15g)

½ a bunch of mint (15g)

1 Peel the garlic, then very finely chop with the anchovies, cornichons and capers, mixing in the mustard to make a paste. Scrape into a bowl.

2 Pick, finely chop and add all the herb leaves. Stir in 1 tablespoon of red wine vinegar and 3 tablespoons of extra virgin olive oil, loosening with little splashes of water to a spoonable consistency. Season to perfection with sea salt and black pepper, and an extra splash of vinegar, to taste.

3 Delicious alongside my Classic leg of lamb (page 144) or Juicy pork belly, fennel & orange salad (page 136). Any leftovers can be stashed in the fridge, where they'll keep happily for up to 2 days.

Salsa rossa piccante

Serves 8 | 25 minutes

4 fresh red chillies

4 red or orange peppers

4 large ripe tomatoes

1 bulb of garlic

1 large red onion

1 teaspoon coriander seeds

1 cinnamon stick

1 lemon

1 bunch of flat-leaf parsley (30g)

1 Light the barbecue (pages 16–19). Prick the chillies and peppers, then place whole on the hot zone with the tomatoes and the whole unpeeled garlic bulb. Halve and add the red onion. Grill until charred and blackened all over, turning with tongs, and removing it all to a large cold cast-iron pan when done. Put the lid on the pan and leave everything to steam for 10 minutes.

2 Meanwhile, in a pestle and mortar, pound the coriander seeds with 1 teaspoon each of sea salt and black pepper until fine.

3 Transfer all the veg to your board, and put the pan on the medium zone. Go in with 2 tablespoons of olive oil and the cinnamon stick. Peel or cut away and discard the charred parts of the red onion, then roughly chop and add to the pan. Squeeze the garlic cloves out of the skins, chop and add to the mix.

4 Peel away the blackened skin from the peppers, chillies and tomatoes, then roughly chop, removing the pepper and chilli seeds and stalks. Add it all to the pan – then, I like to scrape all the seeds and sludge from the board into a bowl and pass it through a sieve into the pan for maximum flavour. Add the coriander seasoning and cook for 10 minutes, stirring regularly, or until soft.

5 Remove from the heat, squeeze in the lemon juice, finely chop and add the parsley leaves and season to perfection. I like to keep it chunky, but you can finely chop it if you prefer. Great with meat, fish, halloumi, chunky veg and flatbreads or my Herby leg of lamb (page 152).

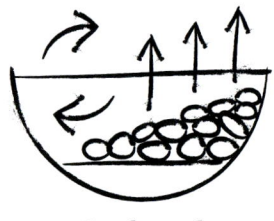

Graduated

Homemade mayo a multitude of ways

Makes 500ml | 15 minutes

1 large egg

1 teaspoon Dijon mustard

500ml light olive oil

½ a lemon

In a large bowl, whisk the egg yolk (save the white for another day). Whisk in the mustard, then, whisking constantly, gradually add drips of the olive oil, moving to a light drizzle then a steady stream, and adding little splashes of red wine vinegar to loosen, if it thickens too much. Season to perfection with sea salt, and a little lemon juice, if needed. It's great as it is, or you can add bonus flavour, as below. Either way, store any excess in a sterilized jar in the fridge for up to 1 week.

Basil mayo

In a pestle and mortar, pound the leaves from **½ a bunch of basil (15g)** into a paste, then muddle in **½ x Homemade mayo** until it becomes a beautiful pale green. Great with my Lemon steamed fish & charred greens (page 36).

Saffron mayo

Put **1 small pinch of saffron** into a small bowl with just **¼ of a teaspoon of boiling water** and leave to infuse for a few minutes. Muddle the saffron water into **½ x Homemade mayo**, until it becomes pale yellow. Lovely with my Sunshine stew & herb-stuffed sea bream (page 54)

Garlic mayo

Place **1 small bulb of garlic** underneath the grill next to the coals and leave to cook in its skin for 1 hour, or until charred but soft in the middle. Or, try throwing a handful of soaked wood chips on the dying embers and leave the garlic to smoke overnight with the lid on, top vent half open. Once cool enough to handle, squeeze out the soft flesh, discarding the skins, then mash and muddle through **½ x Homemade mayo**. Squeeze in a little **lemon juice**, to taste. Brilliant paired with my Skewered sardines on toast (page 68).

Curried mayo

Peel and finely grate **1cm of ginger** into **½ x Homemade mayo**, then muddle in **½ a teaspoon of your favourite curry paste** and squeeze in a little **lemon juice**, to taste. Great with my Grilled chips (page 222).

Smoky ketchup

Makes 350ml | 45 minutes

1 fresh red chilli

2 onions

800g large ripe tomatoes

1 sprig of rosemary

2 cloves of garlic

1 x 460g jar of roasted red peppers

50g soft brown sugar

150ml red wine vinegar

1. Light the barbecue (pages 16–19). Soak a handful of wood chips according to the packet instructions.

2. Prick the chilli, quarter the unpeeled onions, then place them all on the hot zone with the tomatoes. Grill until everything is charred and blackened all over, turning regularly with tongs, and removing to a board once done.

3. Scrape the larger bits of blackened skin off the chilli and tomatoes, deseed the chilli, then roughly chop both. Peel and roughly chop the onions. Scrape it all into a large cast-iron pan, add 2 tablespoons of olive oil, strip in the rosemary leaves, then peel, slice and add the garlic. Drain and tip in the peppers, add a pinch of black pepper and place the pan on the hot zone. Put the drained wood chips alongside, then cook with the barbecue lid on, vents open, for 15 minutes, or until softened.

4. Stir in the sugar, 1 teaspoon of sea salt and the vinegar and simmer for 5 minutes, then, in batches if needed, carefully blitz in a food processor until smooth. Pass through a sieve back into the pan, and simmer until thickened to the consistency of ketchup. Season to perfection, if needed.

5. Leave to cool completely, then use right away, or store in the fridge in sterilized jars or bottles for up to 6 weeks. Once opened, use within 1 week.

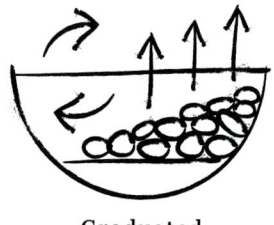

Graduated

Crispy chickpea houmous

Serves 10 | 15 minutes

1 tablespoon cumin seeds

1 x 700g jar of chickpeas

1 tablespoon sesame seeds

1 clove of garlic

2 tablespoons tahini

2 lemons

2 sprigs of thyme or oregano, flowering if you can get it

1 pinch of smoked paprika

1. Toast the cumin seeds in a frying pan over a medium-high heat on the hob, or in a small enamel tray on the hot zone of the barbecue, if you've got it going. Once smelling fantastic, tip half into a small bowl, and half into a blender.

2. Spritz the pan or tray with olive oil, then pat dry and add 4 tablespoons of chickpeas. Fry for 5 minutes, or until golden and crispy, adding the sesame seeds and the cumin from the bowl for the last minute.

3. Tip the rest of the chickpeas, juice and all, into the blender. Peel and add the garlic, along with the tahini, 1 tablespoon of extra virgin olive oil, and a good pinch of sea salt and black pepper. Squeeze in all the lemon juice, then blitz until silky and super-smooth. Taste and adjust the seasoning, if needed.

4. Spoon the houmous into a shallow serving bowl and make a well in the middle. Top with the crispy chickpea mix, pick over the herbs, dust over the paprika, and finish with a drizzle of extra virgin olive oil, if you like.

Charred chilli oil

Makes 1 small jar | 15 minutes, plus cooling

10 fresh mixed-colour chillies

1 teaspoon dried oregano

100ml extra virgin olive oil

When the barbie's lit for a feast, this is one of those fantastic little bonus recipes I love to make on the side, utilizing that grill heat for mega flavour.

1. Light the barbecue (pages 16–19). Prick the chillies, then grill for 5 minutes, or until blackened and softened, turning regularly and removing to a bowl once well charred. Cover, and leave to steam for 5 minutes.

2. Once cool enough to handle, scrape away and discard the chilli skins, seeds and stalks, then chop the soft flesh, mixing it with the oregano as you go.

3. Scrape the chillies into a clean jar, mix with 1 teaspoon each of sea salt and red wine vinegar, then top up with the extra virgin olive oil and stash in the fridge for up to 4 weeks – the longer you leave it, the more the flavours develop. Great with grilled prawns, steak or veggies, and a delight spooned over torn mozzarella on toast with a few fresh herbs and a grating of lemon zest.

Embellish it: I've kept it simple here, but you can absolutely make it your own by adding ingredients like toasted pine nuts, raisins or strips of lemon peel.

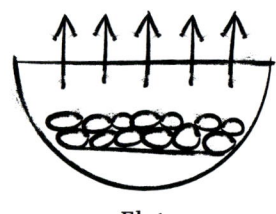

Flat

Bay salt

Makes 1 small jar | 10 minutes

1 tablespoon coriander seeds

1 tablespoon fennel seeds

1 tablespoon garlic granules

6 bay leaves

1 lemon

1 pinch of dried red chilli flakes

A wonderfully fragrant seasoning that can be used to add flavour to all sorts of different meats, fish or veggies prior to cooking or just before serving.

1 Blitz the coriander and fennel seeds, garlic granules and 1 tablespoon of black pepper in a blender until fine, or pound in a pestle and mortar.

2 Tear in the bay, discarding the stalks, use a speed peeler to add the lemon peel in strips, add the chilli flakes and 2 tablespoons of sea salt, then blitz again to incorporate, or pound well if using a pestle and mortar.

3 Use what you need right away in my Ultimate pork ribs (page 158) or Juicy pork belly, fennel & orange salad (page 136), or pop into a jam jar and store in a cool, dark place for up to 1 week.

Mega mac 'n' cheese

Serves 10 as a side | 1 hour

2 onions

2 cloves of garlic

30g unsalted butter

2 bay leaves

½ teaspoon cayenne pepper

50g plain flour

1.2 litres semi-skimmed milk

2 teaspoons English mustard

500g dried macaroni

100g mature Cheddar cheese

100g Red Leicester cheese

100g Parmesan cheese

100g garlic bread

2 sprigs of rosemary

1 Peel and finely chop the onions and garlic, and place in a large ovenproof casserole pan on a medium heat on the hob with the butter, bay, cayenne and 1 tablespoon of olive oil. Cook for 10 minutes, or until softened, stirring occasionally. Stir in the flour for 2 minutes, then gradually stir in the milk and add the mustard. Simmer for 10 minutes, or until thickened, then season to perfection and turn the heat off.

2 Meanwhile, cook the pasta in a large pan of boiling salted water according to the packet instructions, then drain, reserving a mugful of starchy cooking water. Preheat the oven to 180°C.

3 Add the drained pasta to the sauce, grate over all the cheeses, then mix well and season to perfection, if needed. You don't want the sauce to be too thick at this point, so loosen it with a little reserved cooking water, if needed.

4 Tear the garlic bread into a small food processor or blender, strip in the rosemary leaves, and blitz into coarse crumbs. Scatter over the pasta, then carefully transfer to the oven for 30 minutes, or until golden and bubbling. It'll retain its heat for a while, so will sit happily as part of a spread. Yum!

Grilled chips & rosemary salt

Serves 4 as a side | 30 to 40 minutes

1kg Maris Piper potatoes

2 sprigs of rosemary

1 lemon

A grilled chip is a thing of joy. Yes, it requires a bit of love, but it's worth it. After cooking other things, simply shake the coals flat and get grilling.

1. Scrub the potatoes, then slice lengthways into 1cm-thick slabs, using a crinkle-cut knife for added texture, if you've got one. Toss with 2 tablespoons of olive oil and a pinch of black pepper.

2. To make a flavoured salt, strip the rosemary leaves into a pestle and mortar, add 1 teaspoon of sea salt and pound until fine, then finely grate and mix in the lemon zest. Light the barbecue (pages 16–19).

3. Lay all the chips on the grill and cook with the lid on, vents open, for 40 minutes, or until cooked through and charred, turning regularly with tongs and spritzing with oil as you turn them. Remove to a serving dish once done.

4. You can serve the chips right away, or grill them ahead and simply pop them on a metal tray to heat through on the barbecue when you're ready. Sprinkle over some rosemary salt, to taste (saving the rest for another day), and tuck in. Great with my Store-cupboard BBQ sauce (page 202), Chilli sauce (page 204) or any of my flavoured mayos (pages 210), for epic dunking.

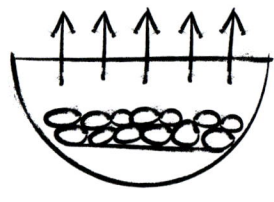

Flat

Beautiful burger buns

Makes 16 | 35 minutes, plus proving & cooling

1kg strong bread flour, plus extra for dusting

1 x 7g sachet of dried yeast

3 large eggs

1 heaped tablespoon runny honey

optional: 2 tablespoons poppy, sesame or fennel seeds

1 Mix the flour, yeast and 20g of sea salt in a large bowl and make a well in the middle. Beat in 2 of the eggs, then add 550ml of lukewarm water and the honey. Mix with a fork, then use clean hands to bring it together into a dough.

2 Knead on a clean, lightly flour-dusted surface for 5 minutes, or until smooth and elastic. Return to a lightly oiled bowl, cover with a clean, damp tea towel and leave in a warm place for 1½ hours, or until doubled in size.

3 Tip out the dough, punch it to knock out the air, then divide into 16 equal pieces. Shape the buns into tight rounds, place on two oiled 25cm x 30cm baking trays, leaving plenty of space between them, cover, and leave for 30 minutes, or until doubled in size again.

4 Preheat the oven to 180°C. Depending on what finish you'd like, either lightly dust the bun tops with flour, or beat the remaining egg, eggwash the buns, and scatter over your chosen seeds. Bake for 25 minutes, or until golden and the bases sound hollow when tapped, then leave to cool completely. Store in an airtight container for up to 3 days, or freeze until needed.

Easy swap: For tasty wholemeal buns, simply swap the strong bread flour for wholemeal bread flour and increase the water to 600ml.

My favourite focaccia

Serves 12 | 45 minutes, plus proving

1 x 7g sachet of dried yeast

1 heaped tablespoon runny honey

1kg strong bread flour, plus extra for dusting

1 In a jug, whisk the yeast into 600ml of lukewarm water, stir in the honey, and leave for 5 minutes. Put the flour and 1 level teaspoon of sea salt into a large bowl and make a well in the middle.

2 Now, gradually pour the yeast mixture into the well, bringing in the flour from the outside to form a dough. Knead on a clean flour-dusted surface for 10 minutes, or until smooth and springy, picking the dough up and slapping it down as you go. Place in a lightly oiled bowl, cover with a clean, damp tea towel, and prove in a warm place for 1 hour, or until doubled in size.

3 Lightly oil a deep roasting tray (30cm x 35cm). Tip in the dough, pull and stretch it out to fill the tray, drizzle with 2 tablespoons of olive oil, then use your fingertips to gently push down and create lots of dips and wells. Sprinkle with a little salt, cover, and leave until doubled in size again.

4 Preheat the oven to 220°C. Very carefully transfer the tray to the bottom of the oven and bake for 25 minutes, or until golden and cooked through. Drizzle with at least 2 tablespoons of extra virgin olive oil, then move to a board, ready to slice and serve.

Get ahead: You can do steps 1 and 2 a day ahead, and simply pop the dough into the fridge overnight.

Embellish it: Team this up with my Arrabiatta chicken drumsticks (page 140) for the most epic sarnie that's sure to go down a treat with your guests.

Charred flatbreads

Serves 4 | 5 minutes

200g self-raising flour, plus extra for dusting

160g natural yoghurt

1. Light the barbecue (pages 16–19) and give the grill a really good brush to clean it – this will help prevent the breads from sticking.

2. In a large bowl, mix the flour with a little pinch of sea salt, the yoghurt and 2 tablespoons of olive oil until it comes together as a dough. Tear equally into four, then flatten out each piece on a clean flour-dusted surface until just under ½cm thick, dusting well with flour as you go.

3. Grill on the hot zone for 1 minute on each side, or until charred, puffed up and cooked through, moving with tongs to the cooler zones, as needed.

Helpful hint: It's really easy to double or triple this recipe to feed a crowd.

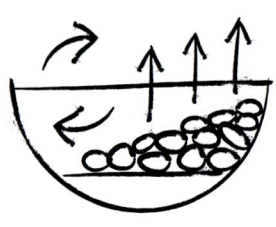

Graduated

Cooking sustainably & kitchen notes

Celebrate quality & seasonality

As is often the case in cooking, using quality ingredients really does make a difference to the success of the recipes. Wherever possible, I've tried to keep the number of ingredients under control, so I'm hoping that will give you the excuse to trade up where you can, buying the best veggies, fish or meat you can find. Also, remember that shopping in season means you get better value for money, and your ingredients will be even more delicious. When it comes to veg and fruit, remember to give everything a nice wash before you start cooking, especially if you're using stuff raw. Other ingredients that are noticeably more delicious when you choose the best quality are: oils and vinegars, sourdough, tinned tomatoes, cheese, beans and chickpeas, jarred and tinned fish, crunchy peanut and sesame chilli oil, sea salt, honey and coffee.

Focusing on fish & seafood

Fish and seafood are an incredibly delicious source of protein, but literally the minute they're caught they start to deteriorate in freshness, so you want to buy them as close to the day of your meal as you can – don't store them in the fridge for days, you're better off with frozen if that's the case. I recommend planning your fish and seafood dinners around your shopping days. Make sure you choose responsibly sourced fish and seafood – look for the MSC logo, or talk to your fishmonger and take their advice. Try to mix up your choices, choosing seasonal, sustainable options as they're available. If you can only find farmed fish, make sure you look for the RSPCA Assured or ASC logo to ensure your fish is responsibly sourced. Jarred and tinned fish are great options, too, particularly when it comes to oily fish.

Meat & eggs

With meat, of course I'm going to endorse higher-welfare farming practices, like organic or free-range. Animals should be raised well, free to roam, display natural behaviours and live a stress-free healthy life. Like most things, you pay more for quality. I'm always a believer that if you take a couple of minutes to plan your weekly menus you can be clever about using cheaper cuts of meat, or you could try cooking some of my meat-reduced and meat-free dishes, which should give you the opportunity to trade up to quality proteins when you do choose them. Butchers can be very helpful – they can order stuff in especially for you and can ensure you have the exact weights you need. Unless essential to a recipe, I try not to specify egg sizes. Hens naturally lay a variety of sizes of egg, so look for mixed-size boxes when shopping to support the best possible welfare standards. Also, with eggs and anything containing egg, such as mayo, always choose free-range or organic.

Dial up your dairy

With staple dairy products, like milk, yoghurt, cottage cheese and butter, please trade up to organic if you can. Every time you buy organic, you vote for a better food system that supports the highest standards of animal welfare, where both cows and land are well looked after.

Bigging up beans

Beans, pulses, chickpeas and lentils are a brilliant and tasty source of plant-based protein: they're budget-friendly, they live happily in the store cupboard for ages, they're easily accessible and they're full of fibre. Plus, they have a wonderful ability to take on flavours from all over the world, and growing beans is actually good for the planet. I've used them throughout this book, and would encourage you to embrace more of them in your cooking. Tinned beans are great, but it's sometimes nice to trade up to jarred beans – they're normally at least twice the price but I'd say they're twice as delicious, too.

Maximizing flavour

In this book I use a lot of what I like to call 'flavour shortcuts': widely available ingredients that allow you to add big bonus flavour, fast, often bolstering the taste of a dish in one super-charged ingredient. Much-loved pastes include rose harissa, miso, gochujang, tahini, chipotle chilli paste and many curry pastes. Useful things in brine include jarred roasted red peppers, jarred sliced jalapeños, pickled walnuts, olives, cornichons and capers. Helpful things in oil: anchovies and sun-dried tomatoes. I love spices and blends like dukkah, dried red chilli flakes, smoked paprika, Cajun seasoning and ground cinnamon, to name a few, as well as nuts, seeds and dried fruit for added crunch and texture; cracking condiments, such as mustards, Marmite, Worcestershire sauce, tomato ketchup, brown sauce, mirin, chilli oils and sauces like sriracha, mango chutney and marmalade, plus super sauces like hoisin, soy and Tabasco. These items guarantee flavour, educate your palate and save hours of time in preparation. Most are non-perishable, which means you're not under pressure to use them up super-quickly.

Bigging up fresh herbs

Fresh herbs are a gift to any cook. Instead of buying them, why not grow them yourself in the garden or in a pot on your windowsill? Herbs allow you to add amazing flavour and fragrance to a dish, without the need to over-season, which is good for everyone. They're also packed with all sorts of incredible qualities on the nutritional front – we like that. And don't forget dried herbs; they're non-perishable and super-convenient to have ready and raring to go in the cupboard.

Fridge organization

When juggling space in the fridge, remember that raw meat and fish should be well wrapped and placed on the bottom shelf to avoid cross-contamination. Any food that is ready to eat, whether it's cooked or it doesn't need to be cooked, should be stored on a higher shelf.

The freezer is your friend

For busy people, without doubt your freezer, if stocked correctly, is your closest ally. There are just a few basic rules when it comes to really utilizing it well. If you're batch-cooking, remember to let food cool thoroughly before freezing – break it down into portions so it cools quicker, and get it into the freezer within 2 hours. Make sure everything is well wrapped, and labelled for future reference. Thaw in the fridge before use, and use within 48 hours. If you've frozen cooked food, don't freeze it again after reheating or defrosting it. You will see me using frozen veg (which I love!) in these recipes – it's super-convenient and widely available. Nutritionally speaking, freezing veg and fruit quickly after harvesting retains the nutritional value very efficiently, often trumping fresh equivalents that have been stuck in the supply chain for a while.

Barbecue & oven lovin'

All recipes were tested on a 57cm charcoal kettle barbecue with two vents – all barbecues are different, so results may vary (for more info, see pages 16–17). Recipes that use an oven were tested in fan ovens – find conversions for conventional, °F and gas online.

A note on nutrition

Our job is to make sure that Jamie can be super-creative, while also ensuring that all recipes meet our guidelines. Every book has a different brief, and *BBQ* is a celebration of recipes you can cook up on your grill. It contains both fun meals for every day and those more indulgent weekend and special occasion dishes perfect for sharing with your loved ones. For clarity and so that you can make informed choices, we've presented easy-to-read nutrition info for each dish on pages 236–240 (displayed per serving). We also want to inspire a more sustainable way of eating, so have included lots of hero veg dishes and meat-free options in this book. Food is fun, joyful and creative – it gives us energy and plays a crucial role in keeping our bodies healthy. Remember, a nutritious, varied and balanced diet and regular exercise are the keys to a healthier lifestyle. We don't label foods as 'good' or 'bad' – there's a place for everything. We encourage an understanding of the difference between nutritious foods for everyday consumption and those to be enjoyed occasionally. For more info about our guidelines and how we analyse recipes, please visit jamieoliver.com/nutrition.

Rozzie Batchelar – Nutritionist, RNutr (food)

A bit about balance

Balance is key when it comes to eating well. Balance your plate right and keep your portion control in check, and you can be confident that you're giving yourself a great start on the path to good health. It's important to consume a variety of foods to ensure we get the nutrients our bodies need to stay healthy. You don't have to be spot-on every day – just try to get your balance right across the week. If you eat meat and fish, as a general guide for main meals you want at least two portions of fish a week, one of which should be oily. Split the rest of the week's main meals between brilliant plant-based meals, some poultry and a little red meat. An all-vegetarian diet can be perfectly healthy, too.

What's the balance?

The UK government's Eatwell Guide shows us what a healthy balance of food looks like. The figures below indicate the proportion of each food group that's recommended across the day.

THE FIVE FOOD GROUPS (UK)	PROPORTION
Vegetables & fruit	40%
Starchy carbohydrates (bread, rice, potatoes, pasta)	38%
Protein (lean meat, fish, eggs, beans, other non-dairy sources)	12%
Dairy foods, milk & dairy alternatives	8%
Unsaturated fats (such as oils)	1%
AND DON'T FORGET TO DRINK PLENTY OF WATER, TOO	

Try to only consume foods and drinks high in fat, salt or sugar occasionally.

Vegetables & fruit

To live a good, healthy life, vegetables and fruit should sit right at the heart of your diet. Veg and fruit come in all kinds of colours, shapes, sizes, flavours and textures, and contain different vitamins and minerals, which each play a part in keeping our bodies healthy and optimal, so variety is key. Eat the rainbow, mixing up your choices as much as you can and embracing the seasons so you're getting produce at its best and its most nutritious. As an absolute minimum, aim for at least 5 portions of fresh, frozen or tinned veg and fruit every day of the week, enjoying more wherever possible. 80g (or a large handful) counts as one portion. You can also count one 30g portion of dried fruit, one 80g portion of beans or pulses, and 150ml of unsweetened veg or fruit juice per day.

Starchy carbohydrates

Carbs provide us with a large proportion of the energy needed to make our bodies move, and to ensure our organs have the fuel they need to function. When you can, choose fibre-rich wholegrain and wholewheat varieties. 260g is the recommended daily amount of carbohydrates for the average adult, with up to 90g coming from total sugars, which includes natural sugars found in whole fruit, milk and milk products, and no more than 30g of free sugars. Free sugars are those added to food and drink, including sugar found in honey, syrups, fruit juice and smoothies. Fibre is classified as a carbohydrate and is mainly found in plant-based foods such as wholegrains, veg and fruit. It helps to keep our digestive systems healthy, control our blood-sugar levels and maintain healthy cholesterol levels. Adults should be aiming for at least 30g of fibre each day.

Protein

Think of protein as the building blocks of our bodies – it's used for everything that's important to how we grow and repair. Try to vary your proteins to include more beans and pulses, two sources of sustainably sourced fish per week (one of which is oily) and reduce red and processed meat if your diet is high in these. Choose lean cuts of animal-based protein where you can. Beans, peas and lentils are great alternatives to meat because they're naturally low in fat and also contain fibre and some vitamins and minerals. Other nutritious protein sources include tofu, eggs, nuts and seeds. Variety is key! The requirement for an average woman aged 19 to 50 is 45g per day, with 55g for men in the same age bracket.

Dairy foods, milk & dairy alternatives

When eaten in the right amounts, this food group offers an amazing array of nutrients. Favour organic dairy milk and yoghurt, and small amounts of cheese, in this category; the lower-fat varieties (with no added sugar) are equally brilliant and worth embracing. If opting for plant-based versions, it's great that we have choice, but it's really important to look for unsweetened fortified options that have added calcium, iodine and vitamin B12 in the ingredients list, to avoid missing out on the key nutrients provided by dairy milk.

Unsaturated fats

While we only need small amounts, we do require healthier fats. Choose unsaturated sources where you can, such as good-quality olive and liquid vegetable oils, nuts, seeds, avocado and omega-3 rich oily fish. Generally speaking, it's recommended that the average woman has no more than 70g of fat per day, with less than 20g of that from saturated fat, and the average man no more than 90g, with less than 30g from saturated fat.

Drink plenty of water

To be the best you can be, stay hydrated. Water is essential to life, and to every function of the human body! In general, women aged 14 and over need at least 2 litres per day, and men in the same age bracket need at least 2.5 litres per day.

Energy & nutrition info

The average woman needs 2,000 calories per day, while the average man needs 2,500. These figures are a rough guide, and what we eat needs to be considered in relation to factors like your age, build, lifestyle and activity levels.

A big thank you

Barbecuing for me is all about forging connections, and there is a wonderful bunch of brilliant people that I'm lucky enough to be connected with in all sorts of different ways, who have supported me in the creation of this beautiful book.

First up, and always leading the way, is my stellar food team. These are the people that live and breathe everything food-related that I do. They soak up inspiration, they share ideas, they help me develop and test recipes, support me on my photo shoots, and are just generally all-round brilliant friends. To my constant support and total trooper, the legend that is Ginny Rolfe, thank you for everything that you do. Big love to my right-hand man Hugo Harrison, and to rising star Isabella Leggett. Much respect for Ben Slater, now off doing his own thing. More respect and all the love to Sharon Sharpe for looking after us all, and to Rebecca Wheeldon and Tilly Wilson for being so helpful behind the scenes. My old-time food teamers, the OGs, Pete Begg and Bobby Sebire, I love you both dearly. Thank you.

I'm lucky to have a wonderful network of talented foodie people that step into the fray to support my core team when we need them to, and that's on everything from chipping into our photo shoots to endless recipe testing to make sure everything is spot on. Big love to Isla Murray, Maddie Rix, Francesca Strange, Sophie Pryn, Chris Nam, Sophie Mackinnon, Steve Pooley, Holly Cowgill and Fran Paling. And to the brilliant runners who helped on our shoots, representing the next generation of talent, thank you Evie Rolfe and Daniel Martin.

Although barbecuing is often about big weekend cookouts, nutrition still has an important part to play, as it does in all the recipes I create. So big love, as always, to Rozzie Batchelar, for helping me make these recipes the best they can be without overstepping any marks! And thank you to Lucinda Cobb for guiding me when it comes to food safety, standards, farming and ethics.

On words, and all the supportive stuff around them, including working with the food team on the mammoth recipe testing process, big love to my extraordinary editor Rebecca Verity, to effervescent Jade Melling and the utterly grill-iant Ruth Tebby, as well as the rest of the mighty editorial team.

And hand-in-hand with words goes design, so sharing much love and respect for my style icon, creative director James Verity, for these beautiful pages, and to the young talent that is Davina Mistry and to the rest of the JO design team.

We had a lot of fun shooting this book, and I think that's reflected in the stunning photography you see in these pages. It comes naturally to my dear friend David Loftus, so thank you, and big love to Richard Bowyer for brilliantly assisting Dave.

I must thank my publishers, the wonderful crew at Penguin Random House. There are so many talented people that work on my books, from creation and printing, to getting them out and seen in the world! I wish I got to spend more time with you all. Big respect to my dear friend, now big boss, Tom Weldon, and to the coolest publisher, the unstoppable Louise Moore. Thank you to Elizabeth Smith, dear Clare Parker, Becca Knight, Rebecca Ogden, Juliette Butler, Katherine Tibbals, Lee Motley, Nick Lowndes, Rachel Myers, Laura Garrod, Beth Stuart, Emma Carter, Hannah Padgham, Chris Wyatt, Tracy Orchard, Chantal Noel, Anjali Nathani, Kate Reiners, Tyra Burr, Joanna Whitehead, Lee-Anne Williams, Jessica Meredeen, George Dimopoulos, Amy Woollard, Sally Hargrave, Stuart Anderson, Jessica Adams, Caroline Newbury, Richard Rowlands and Carrie Anderson. Also to very precious Annie Lee, and to Rachel Malig, Jill Cole and Ruth Ellis.

And over at JO HQ, there is a wonderful bunch of brilliant people, busy doing all sorts of talented things, and they all come together to support these cookbooks. Thank you to the marketing crew, particularly Rosalind Godber and Clare Duffy. Thank you to comms queens Tamsyn Zeitsman and Lydia Waller. Thank you to Rich Herd and the VPU gang, and to Letitia Becher and her social team. Respect to Pamela Lovelock, Therese MacDermott and Mr John Dewar, as well as Timiko Cranwell and team. Thank you to Louise Holland, who goes above and beyond on a daily basis, as does my super-sharp EA Ali Solway. And huge love and gratitude to Zoe Collins x who was by my side at work for 25 years, through thick and thin, and is now off sharing her brilliance with the rest of the world. Lucky them.

There is a luscious complementary TV programme celebrating all things barbecue, that I know you're going to enjoy, so huge thanks to that team. And in particular, the big trio, Sean Moxhay, Sam Beddoes and Katie Millard. As well as Jessica Honeyball, Niall Downing, Giulia Francalanci, Amanda Doig-Moore, Renzo Luzardo, Lulu Welford-Carroll, Prarthana Peterarulthas and all the brilliant crew. The talented Tobie Tripp has again over-delivered on the tunes, and love as always for the teams at Channel 4 and Fremantle. Shout out to Dan Cooper, Jon Folk and Sophie Gudat, talented, good folk from Weber who were brilliant collaborators on the show. Respect, hugs and love for Julia Bell.

And last but never least, the most important people in my life, and the ones that I am lucky enough to share food with every day, my darling family. Huge love for the woman that makes me laugh more than anyone else, my Jools, and to my brilliant children who I'm ever so proud of, Pops, Daisy, Petal, Buddy and River, love you guys. To Mum and Dad, thank you for being just the way you are, and thank you to the rest of the fam. Lastly, to my all-time favourite, Gennaro Contaldo, what would I do without you.

Nutrition

Chicken escalope, smoky bacon & pesto veg — PAGE 24

ENERGY	FAT	SAT FAT	PROTEIN	CARBS	SUGARS	SALT	FIBRE
600kcal	36.9g	7.8g	51.7g	17.6g	7.3g	1.8g	8.7g

Perfect steak & chargrilled salad — PAGE 26

ENERGY	FAT	SAT FAT	PROTEIN	CARBS	SUGARS	SALT	FIBRE
516kcal	24.2g	10.2g	48.1g	29g	22.3g	1g	7.4g

Lamb lollipops, whipped feta & pistachios — PAGE 28

ENERGY	FAT	SAT FAT	PROTEIN	CARBS	SUGARS	SALT	FIBRE
644kcal	33.9g	16.4g	51.6g	35.9g	4g	2.1g	2.7g

Romesco cauliflower — PAGE 30

ENERGY	FAT	SAT FAT	PROTEIN	CARBS	SUGARS	SALT	FIBRE
270kcal	13.1g	2.5g	10.8g	26.8g	12.1g	1g	7.4g

Quick beetroot mackerel — PAGE 32

ENERGY	FAT	SAT FAT	PROTEIN	CARBS	SUGARS	SALT	FIBRE
251kcal	16.4g	4.4g	17.3g	9.1g	7.7g	1.2g	2.6g

Lemon-steamed fish & charred greens — PAGE 36

ENERGY	FAT	SAT FAT	PROTEIN	CARBS	SUGARS	SALT	FIBRE
465kcal	30.9g	3.3g	36.9g	9.4g	5.8g	1.6g	6g

Seared carpaccio of beef — PAGE 38

ENERGY	FAT	SAT FAT	PROTEIN	CARBS	SUGARS	SALT	FIBRE
524kcal	38.4g	11.6g	40.6g	4.1g	3.5g	2.3g	1.8g

Chicken skewers & Tuscan bread salad — PAGE 42

ENERGY	FAT	SAT FAT	PROTEIN	CARBS	SUGARS	SALT	FIBRE
401kcal	14g	7g	35g	36.1g	11.9g	1.3g	5.4g

Grilled fish tacos & stone fruit salsa — PAGE 44

ENERGY	FAT	SAT FAT	PROTEIN	CARBS	SUGARS	SALT	FIBRE
769kcal	39.1g	13.5g	51.6g	55g	18.4g	1.8g	3.9g

Herby aubergine & zingy feta flatbreads — PAGE 46

ENERGY	FAT	SAT FAT	PROTEIN	CARBS	SUGARS	SALT	FIBRE
519kcal	30.8g	9.7g	16g	47.7g	19.2g	2.6g	11.6g

Jools' salmon niçoise — PAGE 48

ENERGY	FAT	SAT FAT	PROTEIN	CARBS	SUGARS	SALT	FIBRE
607kcal	31.4g	5.8g	45.2g	39.3g	8.1g	1.8g	5.4g

Smashed lamb wraps — PAGE 50

ENERGY	FAT	SAT FAT	PROTEIN	CARBS	SUGARS	SALT	FIBRE
728kcal	47.7g	14.1g	34g	41.7g	8.1g	3.7g	4.7g

Citrus chilli tofu, greens & chickpea rice — PAGE 52

ENERGY	FAT	SAT FAT	PROTEIN	CARBS	SUGARS	SALT	FIBRE
571kcal	11.1g	1.6g	25.1g	97.9g	18.1g	0.7g	8.2g

Sunshine stew & herb-stuffed sea bream — PAGE 54

ENERGY	FAT	SAT FAT	PROTEIN	CARBS	SUGARS	SALT	FIBRE
385kcal	18.3g	2.1g	27g	32g	16.9g	1.1g	10g

Chicken shawarma — PAGE 56

ENERGY	FAT	SAT FAT	PROTEIN	CARBS	SUGARS	SALT	FIBRE
434kcal	15.3g	4.3g	36.4g	38.3g	17.5g	1.8g	5.4g

Chicken & chorizo skewers — PAGE 60

ENERGY	FAT	SAT FAT	PROTEIN	CARBS	SUGARS	SALT	FIBRE
238kcal	11.3g	3.3g	23.5g	11.5g	10.3g	1g	2g

Lamb kofta — PAGE 62

ENERGY	FAT	SAT FAT	PROTEIN	CARBS	SUGARS	SALT	FIBRE
435kcal	25g	10.1g	29.9g	22.9g	4.9g	1.6g	2.3g

Halloumi & strawberry skewers — PAGE 64

ENERGY	FAT	SAT FAT	PROTEIN	CARBS	SUGARS	SALT	FIBRE
544kcal	30.2g	19.2g	33.1g	33.6g	5.7g	3.8g	3.6g

Skewered sausages & creamy lentils — PAGE 66

ENERGY	FAT	SAT FAT	PROTEIN	CARBS	SUGARS	SALT	FIBRE
689kcal	46.3g	19.6g	35g	32.8g	9.9g	2.7g	10.4g

Skewered sardines on toast — PAGE 68

ENERGY	FAT	SAT FAT	PROTEIN	CARBS	SUGARS	SALT	FIBRE
449kcal	27g	3.9g	27.9g	22.5g	2g	1.4g	2.4g

Dr Loftus' lamb kebabs — PAGE 70

ENERGY	FAT	SAT FAT	PROTEIN	CARBS	SUGARS	SALT	FIBRE
508kcal	41.4g	13.3g	25.8g	9g	5.9g	0.7g	3.9g

Prawn skewers & ajoblanco sauce — PAGE 72

ENERGY	FAT	SAT FAT	PROTEIN	CARBS	SUGARS	SALT	FIBRE
583kcal	47g	7.5g	28.5g	14.7g	5.3g	1.9g	7.9g

Blushing bavette skewers & ssamjang — PAGE 74

ENERGY	FAT	SAT FAT	PROTEIN	CARBS	SUGARS	SALT	FIBRE
312kcal	17.4g	5.8g	28.2g	11.3g	10.2g	0.5g	2.7g

Sticky sriracha tofu — PAGE 76

ENERGY	FAT	SAT FAT	PROTEIN	CARBS	SUGARS	SALT	FIBRE
552kcal	18.6g	2.7g	21.1g	74.1g	24.6g	2.8g	0.5g

Peanutty chicken skewers — PAGE 78

ENERGY	FAT	SAT FAT	PROTEIN	CARBS	SUGARS	SALT	FIBRE
436kcal	25.9g	10.1g	46.4g	5.5g	3g	1g	1.3g

Spiced pork kebabs — PAGE 80

ENERGY	FAT	SAT FAT	PROTEIN	CARBS	SUGARS	SALT	FIBRE
256kcal	8.8g	3.1g	30g	15.8g	3.4g	0.8g	1.8g

Spiced chicken kebabs & butter sauce — PAGE 82

ENERGY	FAT	SAT FAT	PROTEIN	CARBS	SUGARS	SALT	FIBRE
602kcal	40.1g	19.4g	43g	20g	16.9g	1.5g	3.7g

Coconut & coriander flatbread — PAGE 84

ENERGY	FAT	SAT FAT	PROTEIN	CARBS	SUGARS	SALT	FIBRE
303kcal	10.3g	8g	6.3g	49g	1.9g	1.1g	2.1g

Charred radicchio, orange & burrata salad — PAGE 88

ENERGY	FAT	SAT FAT	PROTEIN	CARBS	SUGARS	SALT	FIBRE
328kcal	23.3g	6.9g	10.7g	20.2g	15.8g	0.6g	4.3g

Grilled caponata — PAGE 90

ENERGY	FAT	SAT FAT	PROTEIN	CARBS	SUGARS	SALT	FIBRE
263kcal	13.6g	4.4g	10.5g	25.4g	7.9g	0.8g	4g

Med-style greens — PAGE 92

ENERGY	FAT	SAT FAT	PROTEIN	CARBS	SUGARS	SALT	FIBRE
125kcal	11.1g	1.6g	2.6g	5.3g	1.7g	1.2g	2g

Sriracha corn — PAGE 94

ENERGY	FAT	SAT FAT	PROTEIN	CARBS	SUGARS	SALT	FIBRE
153kcal	8.1g	0.8g	3.6g	19.8g	7.1g	0.2g	2g

Grilled green grain salad — PAGE 96

ENERGY	FAT	SAT FAT	PROTEIN	CARBS	SUGARS	SALT	FIBRE
296kcal	16.4g	3.6g	11.4g	25.4g	3.2g	0.3g	5.1g

Pickle potato salad — PAGE 98

ENERGY	FAT	SAT FAT	PROTEIN	CARBS	SUGARS	SALT	FIBRE
330kcal	13.5g	6.8g	8.6g	45.7g	8.1g	1.3g	3.4g

Herby grilled carrots & feta — PAGE 100

ENERGY	FAT	SAT FAT	PROTEIN	CARBS	SUGARS	SALT	FIBRE
248kcal	14.4g	4.8g	7.1g	24.6g	14.9g	1.8g	5.3g

Squash, sage & rice salad — PAGE 102

ENERGY	FAT	SAT FAT	PROTEIN	CARBS	SUGARS	SALT	FIBRE
499kcal	13.5g	1.8g	10.9g	89.8g	9.9g	0.4g	5.5g

Courgette & ricotta salad — PAGE 104

ENERGY	FAT	SAT FAT	PROTEIN	CARBS	SUGARS	SALT	FIBRE
113kcal	8.4g	2.9g	4.9g	5.3g	4.7g	0.1g	1.6g

Yoghurt pasta salad — PAGE 106

ENERGY	FAT	SAT FAT	PROTEIN	CARBS	SUGARS	SALT	FIBRE
376kcal	15.7g	4.2g	11.3g	51.5g	4.5g	0.1g	0.7g

Best-ever tomato salad — PAGE 108

ENERGY	FAT	SAT FAT	PROTEIN	CARBS	SUGARS	SALT	FIBRE
100kcal	6.6g	3.2g	4.8g	5.6g	5.5g	0.5g	1.7g

Charred squash & tahini chickpea salad — PAGE 110

ENERGY	FAT	SAT FAT	PROTEIN	CARBS	SUGARS	SALT	FIBRE
195kcal	7.5g	1.5g	7.1g	25.3g	11.3g	0.1g	5.8g

Beautiful Georgian-style stuffed aubergines — PAGE 112

ENERGY	FAT	SAT FAT	PROTEIN	CARBS	SUGARS	SALT	FIBRE
560kcal	51.8g	9.4g	10.1g	19g	9.3g	1.9g	8.5g

Glazed rum pineapple — PAGE 116

ENERGY	FAT	SAT FAT	PROTEIN	CARBS	SUGARS	SALT	FIBRE
309kcal	17.6g	8.8g	4.3g	28.3g	26.9g	0.2g	1.3g

Crispy bacon & sausage sizzlers — PAGE 121

ENERGY	FAT	SAT FAT	PROTEIN	CARBS	SUGARS	SALT	FIBRE
235kcal	18.8g	6.8g	12.4g	4.1g	1.8g	1.3g	1.1g

Dotty coddled egg peppers — PAGE 121

ENERGY	FAT	SAT FAT	PROTEIN	CARBS	SUGARS	SALT	FIBRE
95kcal	5.9g	1.5g	7.1g	4.3g	4.1g	0.4g	2g

Tomato bread — PAGE 122

ENERGY	FAT	SAT FAT	PROTEIN	CARBS	SUGARS	SALT	FIBRE
83kcal	2g	0.3g	2.9g	13.2g	2.3g	0.2g	0.7g

Bubbling baked beans — PAGE 122

ENERGY	FAT	SAT FAT	PROTEIN	CARBS	SUGARS	SALT	FIBRE
168kcal	0.7g	0.1g	10g	32.1g	8.9g	1.3g	8g

Stuffed mushrooms — PAGE 122

ENERGY	FAT	SAT FAT	PROTEIN	CARBS	SUGARS	SALT	FIBRE
104kcal	7.1g	4.4g	7.6g	3.4g	2.3g	0.8g	1.1g

Corn fritters — PAGE 124

ENERGY	FAT	SAT FAT	PROTEIN	CARBS	SUGARS	SALT	FIBRE
342kcal	13g	4.1g	13.3g	44.3g	5.3g	1.5g	2g

BBQ baked beans — PAGE 126

ENERGY	FAT	SAT FAT	PROTEIN	CARBS	SUGARS	SALT	FIBRE
188kcal	5g	0.8g	6.8g	26.9g	15.8g	0.7g	6.4g

Grilled black pepper peaches — PAGE 128

ENERGY	FAT	SAT FAT	PROTEIN	CARBS	SUGARS	SALT	FIBRE
446kcal	16.1g	10.2g	12.7g	64.2g	40.5g	0.7g	3.8g

Halloumi fritters — PAGE 130

ENERGY	FAT	SAT FAT	PROTEIN	CARBS	SUGARS	SALT	FIBRE
254kcal	13.4g	6.3g	15g	38.3g	6.2g	2.2g	1.9g

Barbecued meat chilli — PAGE 134

ENERGY	FAT	SAT FAT	PROTEIN	CARBS	SUGARS	SALT	FIBRE
390kcal	20.6g	7.4g	39.6g	11.8g	5.8g	1.2g	4.2g

Juicy pork belly, fennel & orange salad — PAGE 136

ENERGY	FAT	SAT FAT	PROTEIN	CARBS	SUGARS	SALT	FIBRE
542kcal	42.2g	13.6g	33.4g	8.2g	5.6g	1.5g	2.6g

Gnarly rump steak with salsa, rice & beans — PAGE 138

ENERGY	FAT	SAT FAT	PROTEIN	CARBS	SUGARS	SALT	FIBRE
416kcal	15g	5.9g	30.5g	41.6g	7g	0.9g	3.4g

Arrabiatta chicken drumsticks — PAGE 140

ENERGY	FAT	SAT FAT	PROTEIN	CARBS	SUGARS	SALT	FIBRE
339kcal	15.6g	4g	29.2g	12.2g	10.4g	1g	3.6g

Classic leg of lamb — PAGE 144

ENERGY	FAT	SAT FAT	PROTEIN	CARBS	SUGARS	SALT	FIBRE
487kcal	29.5g	12.2g	44.2g	11.5g	9.2g	1g	3.3g

Herby grilled veg & halloumi skewers — PAGE 146

ENERGY	FAT	SAT FAT	PROTEIN	CARBS	SUGARS	SALT	FIBRE
516kcal	29.1g	7.7g	17.1g	49.6g	18.1g	1.4g	7.7g

Grilled chilli & lemon chicken — PAGE 148

ENERGY	FAT	SAT FAT	PROTEIN	CARBS	SUGARS	SALT	FIBRE
353kcal	20.1g	5g	39.9g	3.1g	1.1g	0.7g	0.6g

Herby leg of lamb & creamy beans — PAGE 152

ENERGY	FAT	SAT FAT	PROTEIN	CARBS	SUGARS	SALT	FIBRE
468kcal	23.2g	8.7g	35.8g	26.7g	3.8g	0.9g	7.5g

Pulled beef tacos — PAGE 154

ENERGY	FAT	SAT FAT	PROTEIN	CARBS	SUGARS	SALT	FIBRE
456kcal	23.1g	6.6g	26.6g	35.9g	13.6g	2.1g	4.5g

Pomegranate & harissa chicken — PAGE 156

ENERGY	FAT	SAT FAT	PROTEIN	CARBS	SUGARS	SALT	FIBRE
395kcal	20.8g	5g	39.6g	12.8g	11.6g	0.8g	1g

Ultimate pork ribs – BBQ sauce glaze — PAGE 158

ENERGY	FAT	SAT FAT	PROTEIN	CARBS	SUGARS	SALT	FIBRE
354kcal	23.4g	10.4g	22.2g	13.6g	12g	2.8g	0.6g

Ultimate pork ribs – hoisin glaze — PAGE 158

ENERGY	FAT	SAT FAT	PROTEIN	CARBS	SUGARS	SALT	FIBRE
387kcal	22.2g	10.2g	21.8g	25.0g	22.8g	2.8g	0.6g

Ultimate pork ribs – mango chutney glaze — PAGE 158

ENERGY	FAT	SAT FAT	PROTEIN	CARBS	SUGARS	SALT	FIBRE
366kcal	22.6g	10.2g	22.2g	18.8g	16.2g	3.3g	1g

Buddy's chicken Caesar — PAGE 160

ENERGY	FAT	SAT FAT	PROTEIN	CARBS	SUGARS	SALT	FIBRE
593kcal	28.3g	9.3g	57.7g	27.1g	10.3g	2.6g	6.7g

Veggie gumbo — PAGE 164

ENERGY	FAT	SAT FAT	PROTEIN	CARBS	SUGARS	SALT	FIBRE
270kcal	10.2g	1.8g	11.6g	35.8g	11.6g	1.4g	9g

Fruity pork chops & grilled potatoes — PAGE 166

ENERGY	FAT	SAT FAT	PROTEIN	CARBS	SUGARS	SALT	FIBRE
709kcal	37.3g	13g	15.2g	48.7g	17.5g	0.9g	4.5g

Super surf & turf mixed grill — PAGE 168

ENERGY	FAT	SAT FAT	PROTEIN	CARBS	SUGARS	SALT	FIBRE
594kcal	36g	11.7g	39g	27.3g	5.1g	2.2g	3.7g

Duck legs & plum sauce — PAGE 170

ENERGY	FAT	SAT FAT	PROTEIN	CARBS	SUGARS	SALT	FIBRE
761kcal	23.6g	7g	50.3g	93.1g	18.1g	2.4g	13.4g

Mint & chilli courgettes — PAGE 174

ENERGY	FAT	SAT FAT	PROTEIN	CARBS	SUGARS	SALT	FIBRE
32kcal	2.4g	0.4g	0.9g	2.3g	1.8g	0g	0.6g

Burnt butter labneh — PAGE 175

ENERGY	FAT	SAT FAT	PROTEIN	CARBS	SUGARS	SALT	FIBRE
163kcal	13.8g	8.6g	4g	5.1g	3.8g	0.5g	1.8g

Anchovies & orange — PAGE 175

ENERGY	FAT	SAT FAT	PROTEIN	CARBS	SUGARS	SALT	FIBRE
11kcal	0.5g	0.1g	1.3g	0.4g	0.4g	0.7g	0g

Halloumi & apricots — PAGE 175

ENERGY	FAT	SAT FAT	PROTEIN	CARBS	SUGARS	SALT	FIBRE
184kcal	13.3g	6.9g	9.7g	7.1g	6.1g	1.1g	1g

Baba ganoush — PAGE 176

ENERGY	FAT	SAT FAT	PROTEIN	CARBS	SUGARS	SALT	FIBRE
53kcal	3.1g	0.5g	2g	5.1g	2.3g	0g	2.9g

Sweet peppers & capers — PAGE 176

ENERGY	FAT	SAT FAT	PROTEIN	CARBS	SUGARS	SALT	FIBRE
17kcal	0.3g	0.1g	0.8g	3g	2.9g	0.2g	1.2g

Tear & share flatbread — PAGE 176

ENERGY	FAT	SAT FAT	PROTEIN	CARBS	SUGARS	SALT	FIBRE
211kcal	3.8g	1.4g	6.7g	39.9g	2.7g	0.8g	1.8g

Paprika pulled pork — PAGE 178

ENERGY	FAT	SAT FAT	PROTEIN	CARBS	SUGARS	SALT	FIBRE
448kcal	33.8g	10.8g	36.2g	0g	0g	0.5g	0g

Gravy cheeseburgers — PAGE 182

ENERGY	FAT	SAT FAT	PROTEIN	CARBS	SUGARS	SALT	FIBRE
764kcal	46.5g	13.3g	41.9g	44.3g	10g	2.9g	3.9g

Miso mushroom burgers — PAGE 184

ENERGY	FAT	SAT FAT	PROTEIN	CARBS	SUGARS	SALT	FIBRE
310kcal	7g	1.1g	11.9g	49.1g	14.4g	2.7g	4.7g

Lamb moussaka burgers — PAGE 188

ENERGY	FAT	SAT FAT	PROTEIN	CARBS	SUGARS	SALT	FIBRE
588kcal	29.3g	14.9g	40.1g	41.4g	10.4g	2.7g	4.6g

Sesame chicken burgers — PAGE 190

ENERGY	FAT	SAT FAT	PROTEIN	CARBS	SUGARS	SALT	FIBRE
438kcal	12.7g	3.1g	38.2g	42.1g	12.1g	1.7g	4.5g

Blue cheese pork burgers — PAGE 192

ENERGY	FAT	SAT FAT	PROTEIN	CARBS	SUGARS	SALT	FIBRE
742kcal	46.2g	15.9g	40.2g	40.5g	11.4g	2.3g	3.2g

Beet & feta bean burgers — PAGE 194

ENERGY	FAT	SAT FAT	PROTEIN	CARBS	SUGARS	SALT	FIBRE
455kcal	9.1g	3.2g	21.4g	71.1g	16.4g	1.8g	10.8g

Prawn toast burgers — PAGE 196

ENERGY	FAT	SAT FAT	PROTEIN	CARBS	SUGARS	SALT	FIBRE
380kcal	8.6g	1.4g	32g	42.6g	12g	1.7g	2.9g

Chorizo fish burgers — PAGE 198

ENERGY	FAT	SAT FAT	PROTEIN	CARBS	SUGARS	SALT	FIBRE
676kcal	38.2g	9.8g	43.5g	39.9g	9.6g	1.9g	4.3g

Store-cupboard BBQ sauce (per tablespoon) — PAGE 202

ENERGY	FAT	SAT FAT	PROTEIN	CARBS	SUGARS	SALT	FIBRE
34kcal	0.6g	0.2g	0.5g	6.4g	5.9g	0.4g	0.2g

Chilli sauce (per tablespoon) — PAGE 204

ENERGY	FAT	SAT FAT	PROTEIN	CARBS	SUGARS	SALT	FIBRE
20kcal	0.9g	0g	0.3g	3.2g	2.9g	0.2g	0.3g

Salsa verde — PAGE 206

ENERGY	FAT	SAT FAT	PROTEIN	CARBS	SUGARS	SALT	FIBRE
60kcal	5.5g	0.8g	1.5g	0.9g	0.6g	0.7g	0.3g

Salsa rossa piccante — PAGE 208

ENERGY	FAT	SAT FAT	PROTEIN	CARBS	SUGARS	SALT	FIBRE
71kcal	3.6g	0.5g	1.9g	8.4g	6.9g	0.5g	2.8g

Homemade mayo (per tablespoon) — PAGE 210

ENERGY	FAT	SAT FAT	PROTEIN	CARBS	SUGARS	SALT	FIBRE
122kcal	13.5g	2g	0.1g	0.1g	0g	0g	0g

Smoky ketchup (per tablespoon) — PAGE 212

ENERGY	FAT	SAT FAT	PROTEIN	CARBS	SUGARS	SALT	FIBRE
33kcal	1g	0g	0.5g	4.9g	4.4g	0.2g	1g

Crispy chickpea houmous — PAGE 214

ENERGY	FAT	SAT FAT	PROTEIN	CARBS	SUGARS	SALT	FIBRE
82kcal	4g	0.6g	3.9g	8g	0.4g	0.2g	2.6g

Charred chilli oil (per tablespoon) — PAGE 216

ENERGY	FAT	SAT FAT	PROTEIN	CARBS	SUGARS	SALT	FIBRE
56kcal	6g	0.9g	0.2g	0.4g	0.4g	0.2g	0.1g

Bay salt (per teaspoon) — PAGE 218

ENERGY	FAT	SAT FAT	PROTEIN	CARBS	SUGARS	SALT	FIBRE
3kcal	0.2g	0g	0.3g	0.5g	0g	1.4g	0.3g

Mega mac 'n' cheese — PAGE 220

ENERGY	FAT	SAT FAT	PROTEIN	CARBS	SUGARS	SALT	FIBRE
419kcal	19g	10.3g	20.6g	55g	9.3g	0.9g	2.7g

Grilled chips & rosemary salt — PAGE 222

ENERGY	FAT	SAT FAT	PROTEIN	CARBS	SUGARS	SALT	FIBRE
247kcal	7.1g	0.9g	5.1g	43.3g	1.5g	1g	3.3g

Beautiful burger buns — PAGE 224

ENERGY	FAT	SAT FAT	PROTEIN	CARBS	SUGARS	SALT	FIBRE
241kcal	1.9g	0.4g	8.8g	50.6g	1.4g	1.3g	2g

My favourite focaccia — PAGE 226

ENERGY	FAT	SAT FAT	PROTEIN	CARBS	SUGARS	SALT	FIBRE
305kcal	3.4g	0.5g	9.8g	62.8g	1.1g	0.3g	2.6g

Charred flatbreads — PAGE 228

ENERGY	FAT	SAT FAT	PROTEIN	CARBS	SUGARS	SALT	FIBRE
252kcal	8.6g	2g	6.1g	39.8g	2.6g	0.8g	1.6g

Index

Recipes marked V are suitable for vegetarians; in some instances you'll need to swap in a vegetarian alternative to cheese such as Parmesan.

A

almonds
    charred squash & tahini chickpea salad — V — 110
    chorizo fish burgers — 198
    prawn skewers & ajoblanco sauce — 72
    romesco cauliflower — V — 30
    squash, sage & rice salad — V — 100
anchovies
    anchovies & orange — 175
    Buddy's chicken Caesar — 160
    classic leg of lamb — 144
    Jools' salmon niçoise — 48
    lemon-steamed fish & charred greens — 36
    salsa verde — 206
    seared carpaccio of beef — 38
    super surf & turf mixed grill — 168
apple juice: chilli sauce — V — 204
apples
    blue cheese pork burgers — 192
    pulled beef tacos — 154
apricots
    fruity pork chops & grilled potatoes — 166
    grilled fish tacos & stone fruit salsa — 44
    halloumi & apricots — V — 175
arrabiatta chicken drumsticks — 140
asparagus
    chicken escalope, smoky bacon, green veg & pesto — 24
    citrus chilli tofu, greens & chickpea rice — V — 52
    grilled green grain salad — V — 96
    lemon-steamed fish & charred greens — 36
    perfect steak & chargrilled salad — 25
aubergines
    baba ganoush — V — 176
    beautiful Georgian-style stuffed aubergines — V — 112
    grilled caponata — V — 90
    herby aubergine & zingy feta flatbreads — V — 46
    herby grilled veg, halloumi skewers & pancakes — V — 146
    lamb moussaka burgers — 188
    sunshine stew & herb-stuffed sea bream — 54
avocado
    corn fritters — V — 124
    grilled green grain salad — V — 96
    miso mushroom burgers — V — 184

B

baba ganoush — V — 176
bacon
    arrabiatta chicken drumsticks — 140
    Buddy's chicken Caesar — 160
    chicken escalope, smoky bacon, green veg & pesto — 24
    chicken skewers & Tuscan bread salad — 42
    crispy bacon & sizzling sausages — 121
    Dr Loftus' lamb kebabs — 70
    gravy cheeseburgers — 182
    pulled beef tacos — 154
    skewered sausages & creamy lentils — 66
baharat seasoning: chicken shawarma — 56
baked beans
    BBQ — V — 126
    bubbling — V — 122
barbecue guide
    chimney starters — 16
    cleaning — 17
    coal set-ups — 18–19
    cooking temperatures — 20
    fuel choice — 16
    preparation and set-up — 12–13
    rôtisserie method — 156
    vents for heat control — 17
barbecued meat chilli — 134
basil
    basil mayo — V — 210
    best-ever tomato salad — V — 108
    chicken skewers & Tuscan bread salad — 42
    corn fritters — V — 124
    courgette & ricotta salad — V — 104
    Med-style greens — V — 92
    salsa verde — 206
    stuffed mushrooms — V — 122
bay leaves
    arrabiatta chicken drumsticks — 140
    bay salt — V — 218
    duck legs & plum sauce — 170
    fruity pork chops & grilled potatoes — 166
    gnarly rump steak with salsa, rice & beans — 138
    grilled chilli & lemon chicken — 148

mega mac 'n' cheese	V	220
pulled beef tacos		154
store-cupboard BBQ sauce		202
bay salt	V	218
duck legs & plum sauce		170
ultimate pork ribs 3 ways		158
BBQ sauce		
BBQ baked beans	V	126
store-cupboard BBQ sauce		202
ultimate pork ribs 3 ways		158
beans		
barbecued meat chilli		134
BBQ baked beans	V	126
beet & feta bean burgers	V	194
bubbling baked beans	V	122
citrus chilli tofu, greens & chickpea rice	V	52
gnarly rump steak with salsa, rice & beans		138
grilled green grain salad	V	96
herby leg of lamb & creamy beans		152
Jools' salmon niçoise		48
lemon-steamed fish & charred greens		36
super surf & turf mixed grill		168
beautiful burger buns	V	224
beautiful Georgian-style stuffed aubergines	V	112
beef		
barbecued meat chilli		134
cooking temperatures		20
gravy cheeseburgers		182
pulled beef tacos		154
seared carpaccio of beef		38
see also steak		
beetroot		
beet & feta bean burgers	V	194
quick beetroot mackerel		32
best-ever tomato salad	V	108
blue cheese pork burgers		192
blushing bavette skewers & ssamjang		74
bread		
beautiful burger buns	V	224
Buddy's chicken Caesar		160
charred flatbreads	V	228
chicken shawarma		56
chicken skewers & Tuscan bread salad		42
coconut & coriander flatbread	V	84
epic chicken arrabiatta sarnie		140
halloumi & strawberry skewers	V	64
herby aubergine & zingy feta flatbreads	V	46
herby leg of lamb & creamy beans		152
lamb kofta		62
mega mac 'n' cheese	V	220
my favourite focaccia	V	226
romesco cauliflower	V	30
skewered sardines on toast		68
smashed lamb wraps		50
super surf & turf mixed grill		168
tear & share flatbread	V	176
tomato bread	V	122
broad beans		
beet & feta bean burgers	V	194
lemon-steamed fish & charred greens		36
broccoli		
Buddy's chicken Caesar		160
citrus chilli tofu, greens & chickpea rice	V	52
grilled green grain salad	V	96
perfect steak & chargrilled salad		25
brown sauce: store-cupboard BBQ sauce		202
brown sugar: smoky ketchup	V	212
bubbling baked beans	V	122
Buddy's chicken Caesar		160
burgers		
beautiful burger buns	V	224
beet & feta bean burgers	V	194
blue cheese pork burgers		192
chorizo fish burgers		198
gravy cheeseburgers		182
lamb moussaka burgers		188
miso mushroom burgers	V	184
prawn toast burgers		196
sesame chicken burgers		190
burnt butter labneh	V	174
burrata: charred radicchio, orange & burrata salad	V	88
butter beans: barbecued meat chilli		134
butternut squash		
charred squash & tahini chickpea salad	V	110
squash, sage & rice salad	V	100

C

cabbage		
blushing bavette skewers & ssamjang		74
Buddy's chicken Caesar		160
chicken shawarma		56
duck legs & plum sauce		170
lemon-steamed fish & charred greens		36
miso mushroom burgers	V	184
pulled beef tacos		154
sesame chicken burgers		190
Cajun seasoning: chicken & chorizo skewers		60

cannellini beans			gravy cheeseburgers		182
gnarly rump steak with salsa, rice & beans		138	grilled black pepper peaches	V	128
herby leg of lamb & creamy beans		152	grilled green grain salad	V	96
capers			halloumi & apricots	V	175
grilled caponata	V	90	halloumi & strawberry skewers	V	64
herby aubergine & zingy feta flatbreads	V	46	halloumi fritters	V	130
Med-style greens	V	92	herby aubergine & zingy feta flatbreads	V	46
salsa verde		206	herby grilled carrots & feta	V	100
sunshine stew & herb-stuffed sea bream		54	herby grilled veg, halloumi skewers & pancakes	V	146
super surf & turf mixed grill		168	lamb lollipops, whipped feta & pistachios		28
sweet peppers & capers	V	176	lamb moussaka burgers		188
carpaccio of beef, seared		38	mega mac 'n' cheese	V	220
carrots			pickle potato salad	V	98
BBQ baked beans	V	126	romesco cauliflower	V	30
blushing bavette skewers & ssamjang		74	stuffed mushrooms	V	122
herby grilled carrots & feta	V	100	chicken		
pulled beef tacos		154	arrabiatta chicken drumsticks		140
cashew nuts: spiced chicken kebabs & butter sauce		82	barbecued meat chilli		134
cauliflower			Buddy's chicken Caesar		160
lemon-steamed fish & charred greens		36	chicken & chorizo skewers		60
romesco cauliflower	V	30	chicken escalope, smoky bacon, green veg & pesto		24
celery			chicken shawarma		56
barbecued meat chilli		134	chicken skewers & Tuscan bread salad		42
BBQ baked beans	V	126	cooking temperatures		20
grilled caponata	V	90	epic chicken arrabiatta sarnie		140
juicy pork belly, fennel & orange salad		136	grilled chilli & lemon chicken		148
skewered sausages & creamy lentils		66	peanutty chicken skewers		78
veggie gumbo	V	164	pomegranate & harissa chicken		156
chard			sesame chicken burgers		190
lemon-steamed fish & charred greens		36	spiced chicken kebabs & butter sauce		82
Med-style greens	V	92	super surf & turf mixed grill		168
skewered sausages & creamy lentils		66	chickpeas		
charred chilli oil	V	216	beet & feta bean burgers	V	194
charred flatbreads	V	228	charred squash & tahini chickpea salad	V	110
charred radicchio, orange & burrata salad	V	88	citrus chilli tofu, greens & chickpea rice	V	52
charred squash & tahini chickpea salad	V	110	crispy chickpea houmous	V	214
cheese			duck legs & plum sauce		170
beautiful Georgian-style stuffed aubergines	V	112	veggie gumbo	V	164
beet & feta bean burgers	V	194	chicory: charred radicchio, orange & burrata salad	V	88
best-ever tomato salad	V	108	chilli, barbecued meat		134
blue cheese pork burgers		192	chilli jam		
Buddy's chicken Caesar		160	corn fritters	V	124
charred radicchio, orange & burrata salad	V	88	prawn toast burgers		196
chicken escalope, smoky bacon, green veg & pesto		24	chilli oil		
chicken skewers & Tuscan bread salad		42	charred chilli oil	V	216
chorizo fish burgers		198	citrus chilli tofu, greens & chickpea rice	V	52
courgette & ricotta salad	V	104	corn fritters	V	124
epic chicken arrabiatta sarnie		140			

chillies		
arrabiatta chicken drumsticks		140
Buddy's chicken Caesar		160
charred chilli oil	V	216
chilli sauce	V	204
grilled chilli & lemon chicken		148
grilled fish tacos & stone fruit salsa		44
grilled green grain salad	V	96
halloumi fritters	V	130
herby grilled veg, halloumi skewers & pancakes	V	146
juicy pork belly, fennel & orange salad		136
mint & chilli courgettes	V	174
peanutty chicken skewers		78
prawn toast burgers		196
salsa rossa picante	V	208
seared carpaccio of beef		38
smoky ketchup	V	212
spiced chicken kebabs & butter sauce		82
spiced pork kebabs		80
veggie gumbo	V	164
chillies, pickled: smashed lamb wraps		50
chimney starters		16
chipotle chilli paste: barbecued meat chilli		134
chives		
blue cheese pork burgers		192
Jools' salmon niçoise		48
chorizo		
chicken & chorizo skewers		60
chorizo fish burgers		198
gnarly rump steak with salsa, rice & beans		138
prawn skewers & ajoblanco sauce		72
super surf & turf mixed grill		168
cider: ultimate pork ribs 3 ways		158
cider vinegar		
chilli sauce	V	204
spiced pork kebabs		80
citrus chilli tofu, greens & chickpea rice	V	52
clams: super surf & turf mixed grill		168
classic leg of lamb		144
cleaning the grill		17
clementines		
charred radicchio, orange & burrata salad	V	88
charred squash & tahini chickpea salad	V	110
herby grilled carrots & feta	V	100
coal set-ups		18–19
coconut cream: peanutty chicken skewers		78
coconut milk: coconut & coriander flatbread	V	84
coffee: barbecued meat chilli		134
cooking temperatures		20

coriander		
barbecued meat chilli		134
coconut & coriander flatbread	V	84
grilled fish tacos & stone fruit salsa		44
peanutty chicken skewers		78
prawn toast burgers		196
sticky sriracha tofu	V	76
corn fritters	V	124
corn on the cob		
sriracha corn	V	94
veggie gumbo	V	164
cornichons		
blue cheese pork burgers		192
pickle potato salad	V	98
salsa verde		206
cottage cheese: corn fritters	V	124
courgettes		
chicken skewers & Tuscan bread salad		42
courgette & ricotta salad	V	104
Dr Loftus' lamb kebabs		70
herby grilled veg, halloumi skewers & pancakes	V	146
Jools' salmon niçoise		48
mint & chilli courgettes	V	174
sunshine stew & herb-stuffed sea bream		54
cranberries		
herby grilled veg, halloumi skewers & pancakes	V	146
squash, sage & rice salad	V	100
cream		
skewered sausages & creamy lentils		66
spiced chicken kebabs & butter sauce		82
crème fraîche: blue cheese pork burgers		192
crispy bacon & sizzling sausages		121
crispy chickpea houmous	V	214
cucumber		
blushing bavette skewers & ssamjang		74
gravy cheeseburgers		182
halloumi & strawberry skewers	V	64
halloumi fritters	V	130
lamb kofta		62
miso mushroom burgers	V	184
prawn toast burgers		196
sesame chicken burgers		190
smashed lamb wraps		50
sticky sriracha tofu	V	76
curried mayo	V	210

D

damsons: grilled fish tacos & stone fruit salsa		44
dill: pickle potato salad	V	98
dotty coddled egg peppers	V	121
Dr Loftus' lamb kebabs		70
duck legs & plum sauce		170
dukkah		
burnt butter labneh	V	175
charred squash & tahini chickpea salad	V	110

E

eggs		
beautiful burger buns	V	224
corn fritters	V	124
dotty coddled egg peppers	V	121
halloumi fritters	V	130
homemade mayo, a multitude of ways	V	210
Jools' salmon niçoise		48
epic chicken arrabiatta sarnie		140

F

fennel		
herby grilled veg, halloumi skewers & pancakes	V	146
juicy pork belly, fennel & orange salad		136
super surf & turf mixed grill		168
fennel seeds		
bay salt	V	218
lamb lollipops, whipped feta & pistachios		28
seared carpaccio of beef		38
sunshine stew & herb-stuffed sea bream		54
yoghurt pasta salad	V	106
feta cheese		
beautiful Georgian-style stuffed aubergines	V	112
beet & feta bean burgers	V	194
chicken escalope, smoky bacon, green veg & pesto		24
grilled green grain salad	V	96
herby aubergine & zingy feta flatbreads	V	46
herby grilled carrots & feta	V	100
lamb lollipops, whipped feta & pistachios		28
lamb moussaka burgers		188
pickle potato salad	V	98
romesco cauliflower	V	30
fish		
Buddy's chicken Caesar		160
chorizo fish burgers		198
classic leg of lamb		144
cooking temperatures		20
grilled fish tacos & stone fruit salsa		44
Jools' salmon niçoise		48
lemon-steamed fish & charred greens		36
quick beetroot mackerel		32
salsa verde		206
seared carpaccio of beef		38
skewered sardines on toast		68
sunshine stew & herb-stuffed sea bream		54
super surf & turf mixed grill		168
focaccia, my favourite	V	226
French beans: Jools' salmon niçoise		48
fruity pork chops & grilled potatoes		166

G

garlic		
classic leg of lamb		144
garlic mayo	V	210
grilled chilli & lemon chicken		148
lamb lollipops, whipped feta & pistachios		28
salsa rossa picante	V	208
ginger		
citrus chilli tofu, greens & chickpea rice	V	52
curried mayo	V	210
perfect steak & chargrilled salad		25
prawn toast burgers		196
spiced chicken kebabs & butter sauce		82
spiced pork kebabs		80
sticky sriracha tofu	V	76
glazed rum pineapple	V	116
gnarly rump steak with salsa, rice & beans		138
gochujang paste: sesame chicken burgers		190
grains: grilled green grain salad	V	96
grapefruit: citrus chilli tofu, greens & chickpea rice	V	52
gravy cheeseburgers		182
green beans		
citrus chilli tofu, greens & chickpea rice	V	52
grilled green grain salad	V	96
super surf & turf mixed grill		168
grilled black pepper peaches	V	128
grilled caponata	V	90
grilled chilli & lemon chicken		148
grilled chips & rosemary salt	V	222
grilled fish tacos & stone fruit salsa		44
grilled green grain salad	V	96
gumbo, veggie	V	164

H

halloumi
- halloumi & apricots V 175
- halloumi & strawberry skewers V 64
- halloumi fritters V 130
- herby grilled veg, halloumi skewers & pancakes V 146
- stuffed mushrooms V 122

harissa: pomegranate & harissa chicken 156

hazelnuts
- charred radicchio, orange & burrata salad V 88
- yoghurt pasta salad V 106

herbs
- anchovies & orange 175
- beet & feta bean burgers V 194
- Buddy's chicken Caesar 160
- charred squash & tahini chickpea salad V 110
- Dr Loftus' lamb kebabs 70
- duck legs & plum sauce 170
- halloumi & strawberry skewers V 64
- herby grilled veg, halloumi skewers & pancakes V 146
- herby leg of lamb & creamy beans 152
- juicy pork belly, fennel & orange salad 136
- lamb kofta 62
- lemon-steamed fish & charred greens 36
- perfect steak & chargrilled salad 25
- pulled beef tacos 154
- seared carpaccio of beef 38
- spiced pork kebabs 80
- sunshine stew & herb-stuffed sea bream 54
- super surf & turf mixed grill 168
- *see also* specific herbs

herby aubergine & zingy feta flatbreads 46
herby grilled carrots & feta V 100
hoisin sauce: ultimate pork ribs 3 ways 158
homemade mayo, a multitude of ways V 210

honey
- beautiful burger buns V 224
- blushing bavette skewers & ssamjang 74
- charred radicchio, orange & burrata salad V 88
- chicken & chorizo skewers 60
- chilli sauce V 204
- citrus chilli tofu, greens & chickpea rice V 52
- fruity pork chops & grilled potatoes 166
- glazed rum pineapple V 116
- grilled black pepper peaches V 128
- halloumi & apricots V 175
- herby aubergine & zingy feta flatbreads V 46

herby grilled carrots & feta V 100
herby grilled veg, halloumi skewers & pancakes V 146
my favourite focaccia V 226
perfect steak & chargrilled salad 25
pomegranate & harissa chicken 156
sticky sriracha tofu V 76

horseradish
- gravy cheeseburgers 182
- quick beetroot mackerel 32

houmous, crispy chickpea V 214

J

jalapeños
- barbecued meat chilli 134
- corn fritters V 124

Jools' salmon niçoise 48
juicy pork belly, fennel & orange salad 136

K

ketchup
- smoky ketchup V 212
- store-cupboard BBQ sauce 202

kofta, lamb 62

L

labneh
- burnt butter labneh V 175
- charred squash & tahini chickpea salad V 110

lamb
- classic leg of lamb 144
- cooking temperatures 20
- Dr Loftus' lamb kebabs 70
- herby leg of lamb & creamy beans 152
- lamb kofta 62
- lamb lollipops, whipped feta & pistachios 28
- lamb moussaka burgers 188
- smashed lamb wraps 50

lemons
- arrabiatta chicken drumsticks 140
- baba ganoush V 176
- bay salt V 218
- beautiful Georgian-style stuffed aubergines V 112
- blue cheese pork burgers 192
- Buddy's chicken Caesar 160
- burnt butter labneh V 175

charred squash & tahini chickpea salad	V	110
chicken escalope, smoky bacon, green veg & pesto		24
chicken shawarma		56
chicken skewers & Tuscan bread salad		42
chorizo fish burgers		198
classic leg of lamb		144
coconut & coriander flatbread	V	84
courgette & ricotta salad	V	104
crispy chickpea houmous	V	214
Dr Loftus' lamb kebabs		70
grilled black pepper peaches	V	128
grilled caponata	V	90
grilled chilli & lemon chicken		148
grilled chips & rosemary salt	V	222
grilled green grain salad	V	96
halloumi & strawberry skewers	V	64
halloumi fritters	V	130
herby aubergine & zingy feta flatbreads	V	46
herby grilled veg, halloumi skewers & pancakes	V	146
herby leg of lamb & creamy beans		152
homemade mayo, a multitude of ways	V	210
Jools' salmon niçoise		48
juicy pork belly, fennel & orange salad		136
lamb kofta		62
lamb lollipops, whipped feta & pistachios		28
lemon-steamed fish & charred greens		36
Med-style greens	V	92
pickle potato salad	V	98
pomegranate & harissa chicken		156
prawn skewers & ajoblanco sauce		72
quick beetroot mackerel		32
salsa rossa picante	V	208
seared carpaccio of beef		38
skewered sardines on toast		68
spiced chicken kebabs & butter sauce		82
squash, sage & rice salad	V	100
store-cupboard BBQ sauce		202
stuffed mushrooms	V	122
sunshine stew & herb-stuffed sea bream		54
super surf & turf mixed grill		168
sweet peppers & capers	V	176
yoghurt pasta salad	V	106
lentils: skewered sausages & creamy lentils		66
lettuce		
blue cheese pork burgers		192
blushing bavette skewers & ssamjang		74
Buddy's chicken Caesar		160
charred radicchio, orange & burrata salad	V	88
chicken escalope, smoky bacon, green veg & pesto		24
limes		
blushing bavette skewers & ssamjang		74
chicken & chorizo skewers		60
citrus chilli tofu, greens & chickpea rice	V	52
corn fritters	V	124
glazed rum pineapple	V	116
grilled fish tacos & stone fruit salsa		44
miso mushroom burgers	V	184
peanutty chicken skewers		78
perfect steak & chargrilled salad		25
prawn toast burgers		196
pulled beef tacos		154
sesame chicken burgers		190
sriracha corn	V	94
linseeds: herby grilled carrots & feta	V	100

M

mac 'n' cheese, mega	V	220
mackerel		
grilled fish tacos & stone fruit salsa		44
quick beetroot mackerel		32
mangetout: lemon-steamed fish & charred greens		36
mango chutney: ultimate pork ribs 3 ways		158
maple syrup: miso mushroom burgers	V	184
marmalade		
pulled beef tacos		154
store-cupboard BBQ sauce		202
Marmite		
gravy cheeseburgers		182
store-cupboard BBQ sauce		202
mayonnaise		
gravy cheeseburgers		182
homemade mayo, a multitude of ways	V	210
lemon-steamed fish & charred greens		36
seared carpaccio of beef		38
skewered sardines on toast		68
sriracha corn	V	94
Med-style greens	V	92
mega mac 'n' cheese	V	220
mezze, veg-tastic barbecue		173–6
milk: mega mac 'n' cheese	V	220
mint		
gnarly rump steak with salsa, rice & beans		138
grilled green grain salad	V	96
halloumi fritters	V	130
herby aubergine & zingy feta flatbreads	V	46
lamb kofta		62

lamb lollipops, whipped feta & pistachios		28
mint & chilli courgettes	V	174
perfect steak & chargrilled salad		25
salsa verde		206
sesame chicken burgers		190
smashed lamb wraps		50
yoghurt pasta salad	V	106
mirin: miso mushroom burgers	V	184
miso mushroom burgers	V	184
mixed grill, super surf & turf		168
mushrooms		
Dr Loftus' lamb kebabs		70
miso mushroom burgers	V	184
sticky sriracha tofu	V	76
stuffed mushrooms	V	122
mussels: super surf & turf mixed grill		168
mustard		
blue cheese pork burgers		192
Buddy's chicken Caesar		160
Dr Loftus' lamb kebabs		70
gravy cheeseburgers		182
herby leg of lamb & creamy beans		152
homemade mayo, a multitude of ways	V	210
Jools' salmon niçoise		48
mega mac 'n' cheese	V	220
prawn toast burgers		196
pulled beef tacos		154
salsa verde		206
seared carpaccio of beef		38
skewered sausages & creamy lentils		66
store-cupboard BBQ sauce		202
my favourite focaccia	V	226

N

noodles: sticky sriracha tofu	V	76
nutrition		232–3
nuts		
herby grilled veg, halloumi skewers & pancakes	V	146
see also specific nuts		

O

oil, charred chilli	V	216
okra: veggie gumbo	V	164
Old Bay seasoning: veggie gumbo	V	164
olives		
grilled caponata	V	90
halloumi fritters	V	130
Jools' salmon niçoise		48
juicy pork belly, fennel & orange salad		136
Med-style greens	V	92
sunshine stew & herb-stuffed sea bream		54
sweet peppers & capers	V	176
onions		
arrabiatta chicken drumsticks		140
BBQ baked beans	V	126
chicken & chorizo skewers		60
chicken shawarma		56
classic leg of lamb		144
crispy bacon & sizzling sausages		121
Dr Loftus' lamb kebabs		70
gnarly rump steak with salsa, rice & beans		138
gravy cheeseburgers		182
grilled caponata	V	90
herby grilled veg, halloumi skewers & pancakes	V	146
lamb kofta		62
mega mac 'n' cheese	V	220
pickle potato salad	V	98
pomegranate & harissa chicken		156
pulled beef tacos		154
salsa rossa picante	V	208
skewered sausages & creamy lentils		66
smoky ketchup	V	212
spiced chicken kebabs & butter sauce		82
spiced pork kebabs		80
sunshine stew & herb-stuffed sea bream		54
veggie gumbo	V	164
oranges		
anchovies & orange		175
charred radicchio, orange & burrata salad	V	88
charred squash & tahini chickpea salad	V	110
citrus chilli tofu, greens & chickpea rice	V	52
juicy pork belly, fennel & orange salad		136
ultimate pork ribs 3 ways		158
oregano		
charred chilli oil	V	216
crispy chickpea houmous	V	214
grilled caponata	V	90

P

pak choi: citrus chilli tofu, greens & chickpea rice	V	52
pancakes: herby grilled veg, halloumi skewers & pancakes	V	146
panettone: grilled black pepper peaches	V	128
paprika pulled pork		178

parsley		
baba ganoush	V	176
chicken escalope, smoky bacon,		
green veg & pesto		24
chicken shawarma		56
chorizo fish burgers		198
gravy cheeseburgers		182
grilled caponata	V	90
grilled green grain salad	V	96
herby aubergine & zingy feta flatbreads	V	46
herby grilled carrots & feta	V	100
lamb moussaka burgers		188
prawn skewers & ajoblanco sauce		72
romesco cauliflower	V	30
salsa rossa picante	V	208
salsa verde		206
skewered sardines on toast		68
veggie gumbo	V	164
pasta		
mega mac 'n' cheese	V	220
yoghurt pasta salad	V	106
peaches		
fruity pork chops & grilled potatoes		166
grilled black pepper peaches	V	128
peanuts		
glazed rum pineapple	V	116
peanutty chicken skewers		78
sticky sriracha tofu	V	76
pears: juicy pork belly, fennel & orange salad		136
peas: chicken escalope, smoky bacon,		
green veg & pesto		24
peppers		
barbecued meat chilli		134
chicken & chorizo skewers		60
chicken skewers & Tuscan bread salad		42
chilli sauce	V	204
chorizo fish burgers		198
dotty coddled egg peppers	V	121
Dr Loftus' lamb kebabs		70
gnarly rump steak with salsa, rice & beans		138
herby grilled veg, halloumi skewers & pancakes	V	146
salsa rossa picante	V	208
sesame chicken burgers		190
skewered sausages & creamy lentils		66
sunshine stew & herb-stuffed sea bream		54
sweet peppers & capers	V	176
veggie gumbo	V	164
peppers, padrón		
prawn skewers & ajoblanco sauce		72
sweet peppers & capers	V	176
peppers, roasted		
BBQ baked beans	V	126
romesco cauliflower	V	30
smoky ketchup	V	212
perfect steak & chargrilled salad		25
pickle potato salad	V	98
pine nuts		
grilled caponata	V	90
yoghurt pasta salad	V	106
pineapple		
chicken shawarma		56
glazed rum pineapple	V	116
gnarly rump steak with salsa, rice & beans		138
spiced chicken kebabs & butter sauce		82
pistachios		
chicken escalope, smoky bacon,		
green veg & pesto		24
courgette & ricotta salad	V	104
herby aubergine & zingy feta flatbreads	V	46
herby leg of lamb & creamy beans		152
lamb lollipops, whipped feta & pistachios		28
plums		
duck legs & plum sauce		170
fruity pork chops & grilled potatoes		166
grilled fish tacos & stone fruit salsa		44
pomegranate		
beautiful Georgian-style stuffed aubergines	V	112
charred squash & tahini chickpea salad	V	110
herby aubergine & zingy feta flatbreads	V	46
herby grilled veg, halloumi skewers & pancakes	V	146
pomegranate & harissa chicken		156
ultimate pork ribs 3 ways		158
pork		
barbecued meat chilli		134
blue cheese pork burgers		192
cooking temperatures		20
fruity pork chops & grilled potatoes		166
juicy pork belly, fennel & orange salad		136
paprika pulled pork		178
spiced pork kebabs		80
ultimate pork ribs 3 ways		158
potatoes		
fruity pork chops & grilled potatoes		166
grilled chips & rosemary salt	V	222
Jools' salmon niçoise		48
lamb lollipops, whipped feta & pistachios		28
pickle potato salad	V	98
spiced pork kebabs		80
sunshine stew & herb-stuffed sea bream		54
prawns		
prawn skewers & ajoblanco sauce		72

prawn toast burgers		196
super surf & turf mixed grill		168
pulled beef tacos		154
pumpkin seeds		
grilled green grain salad	V	96
herby grilled carrots & feta	V	100

Q

quick beetroot mackerel		32
quinoa: beet & feta bean burgers	V	194

R

radicchio: charred radicchio orange & burrata salad	V	88
radishes		
blushing bavette skewers & ssamjang		74
perfect steak & chargrilled salad		25
smashed lamb wraps		50
sticky sriracha tofu	V	76
ribs: ultimate pork ribs 3 ways		158
rice		
citrus chilli tofu, greens & chickpea rice	V	52
duck legs & plum sauce		170
gnarly rump steak with salsa, rice & beans		138
squash, sage & rice salad	V	100
ricotta cheese		
chicken skewers & Tuscan bread salad		42
courgette & ricotta salad	V	104
grilled black pepper peaches	V	128
rocket		
gnarly rump steak with salsa, rice & beans		138
seared carpaccio of beef		38
romesco cauliflower	V	30
rosemary		
charred radicchio, orange & burrata salad	V	88
gnarly rump steak with salsa, rice & beans		138
grilled chips & rosemary salt	V	222
mega mac 'n' cheese	V	220
skewered sausages & creamy lentils		66
rôtisserie method		156
rum: glazed rum pineapple	V	116

S

saffron mayo	V	210
sage		
BBQ baked beans	V	126
classic leg of lamb		144
crispy bacon & sizzling sausages		121
fruity pork chops & grilled potatoes		166
herby leg of lamb & creamy beans		152
squash, sage & rice salad	V	100
salads		
best-ever tomato salad	V	108
Buddy's chicken Caesar		160
charred radicchio, orange & burrata salad	V	88
charred squash & tahini chickpea salad	V	110
courgette & ricotta salad	V	104
grilled caponata	V	90
grilled green grain salad	V	96
herby grilled carrots & feta	V	100
Jools' salmon niçoise		48
juicy pork belly, fennel & orange salad		136
Med-style greens	V	92
perfect steak & chargrilled salad		25
pickle potato salad	V	98
squash, sage & rice salad	V	100
sriracha corn	V	94
yoghurt pasta salad	V	106
salmon: Jools' salmon niçoise		48
salsa rossa picante	V	208
salsa verde		206
sardines: skewered sardines on toast		68
sauces		
chilli sauce	V	204
salsa rossa picante	V	208
salsa verde		206
smoky ketchup	V	212
store-cupboard BBQ sauce		202
see also mayonnaise		
sausages		
cooking temperatures		20
crispy bacon & sizzling sausages		121
skewered sausages & creamy lentils		66
scallops: grilled fish tacos & stone fruit salsa		44
sea bass: lemon-steamed fish & charred greens		36
sea bream: sunshine stew & herb-stuffed sea bream		54
seared carpaccio of beef		38
sesame seeds		
crispy chickpea houmous	V	214
prawn toast burgers		196
sesame chicken burgers		190
tear & share flatbread	V	176
shawarma, chicken		56
skewered sardines on toast		68
skewered sausages & creamy lentils		66
smashed lamb wraps		50

smoky ketchup	V	212
soured cream		
grilled fish tacos & stone fruit salsa		44
pickle potato salad	V	98
soy sauce		
blushing bavette skewers & ssamjang		74
citrus chilli tofu, greens & chickpea rice	V	52
miso mushroom burgers	V	184
peanutty chicken skewers		78
perfect steak & chargrilled salad		25
sticky sriracha tofu	V	76
spiced chicken kebabs & butter sauce		82
spring onions		
baba ganoush	V	176
barbecued meat chilli		134
chicken escalope, smoky bacon, green veg & pesto		24
fruity pork chops & grilled potatoes		166
grilled fish tacos & stone fruit salsa		44
halloumi fritters	V	130
lamb moussaka burgers		188
lemon-steamed fish & charred greens		36
miso mushroom burgers	V	184
perfect steak & chargrilled salad		25
prawn toast burgers		196
sesame chicken burgers		190
sriracha corn	V	94
super surf & turf mixed grill		168
veggie gumbo	V	164
squash		
charred squash & tahini chickpea salad	V	110
squash, sage & rice salad	V	100
sriracha chilli sauce		
sriracha corn	V	94
sticky sriracha tofu	V	76
ssamjang: blushing bavette skewers & ssamjang		74
steak		
barbecued meat chilli		134
blushing bavette skewers & ssamjang		74
cooking temperatures		20
gnarly rump steak with salsa, rice & beans		138
perfect steak & chargrilled salad		25
stem ginger syrup: store-cupboard BBQ sauce		202
sticky sriracha tofu	V	76
Stilton cheese: blue cheese pork burgers		192
store-cupboard BBQ sauce		202
strawberries: halloumi & strawberry skewers	V	64
stuffed mushrooms	V	122
sugar snap peas: perfect steak & chargrilled salad		25
sumac: lamb kofta		62
sunflower seeds: herby grilled carrots & feta	V	100
sunshine stew & herb-stuffed sea bream		54
super surf & turf mixed grill		168
sweet peppers & capers	V	176
sweetcorn: corn fritters	V	124

T

tacos		
grilled fish tacos & stone fruit salsa		44
pulled beef tacos		154
tahini		
baba ganoush	V	176
charred squash & tahini chickpea salad	V	110
crispy chickpea houmous	V	214
tarragon: beautiful Georgian-style stuffed aubergines	V	112
tear & share flatbread	V	176
Thai curry paste: peanutty chicken skewers		78
thyme		
burnt butter labneh	V	175
charred radicchio, orange & burrata salad	V	88
crispy chickpea houmous	V	214
glazed rum pineapple	V	116
grilled chilli & lemon chicken		148
grilled fish tacos & stone fruit salsa		44
halloumi & apricots	V	175
quick beetroot mackerel		32
tofu		
citrus chilli tofu, greens & chickpea rice	V	52
sticky sriracha tofu		76
tomato ketchup: store-cupboard BBQ sauce		202
tomato purée		
arrabiatta chicken drumsticks		140
skewered sausages & creamy lentils		66
tomatoes		
arrabiatta chicken drumsticks		140
barbecued meat chilli		134
BBQ baked beans	V	126
best-ever tomato salad	V	108
chicken shawarma		56
chicken skewers & Tuscan bread salad		42
chilli sauce	V	204
classic leg of lamb		144
corn fritters	V	124
courgette & ricotta salad	V	104
dotty coddled egg peppers	V	121
Dr Loftus' lamb kebabs		70
gnarly rump steak with salsa, rice & beans		138
gravy cheeseburgers		182

grilled caponata	V	90
herby grilled veg, halloumi skewers & pancakes	V	146
herby leg of lamb & creamy beans		152
lamb moussaka burgers		188
Med-style greens	V	92
romesco cauliflower	V	30
salsa rossa picante	V	208
seared carpaccio of beef		38
smoky ketchup	V	212
spiced chicken kebabs & butter sauce		82
sunshine stew & herb-stuffed sea bream		54
super surf & turf mixed grill		168
tomato bread	V	122
veggie gumbo	V	164
tomatoes, sun-dried: smashed lamb wraps		50
tortillas		
grilled fish tacos & stone fruit salsa		44
pulled beef tacos		154
smashed lamb wraps		50
trout: grilled fish tacos & stone fruit salsa		44

U

ultimate barbecue brekkie	118–23
ultimate pork ribs 3 ways	158

V

veg-tastic barbecue mezze		173–6
veggie gumbo	V	164
vents for heat control		17
vodka: arrabiatta chicken drumsticks		140

W

walnuts		
beautiful Georgian-style stuffed aubergines	V	112
blue cheese pork burgers		192
walnuts, pickled: pulled beef tacos		154
watercress: pulled beef tacos		154
watermelon: halloumi fritters	V	130
whisky: fruity pork chops & grilled potatoes		166
wine		
store-cupboard BBQ sauce		202
super surf & turf mixed grill		168
Worcestershire sauce		
Buddy's chicken Caesar		160
pulled beef tacos		154
store-cupboard BBQ sauce		202

Y

yoghurt		
beautiful Georgian-style stuffed aubergines	V	112
beet & feta bean burgers	V	194
Buddy's chicken Caesar		160
burnt butter labneh	V	175
charred flatbreads	V	228
charred squash & tahini chickpea salad	V	110
chicken shawarma		56
corn fritters	V	124
duck legs & plum sauce		170
glazed rum pineapple	V	116
herby grilled veg, halloumi skewers & pancakes	V	146
lamb kofta		62
pickle potato salad	V	98
prawn toast burgers		196
quick beetroot mackerel		32
sesame chicken burgers		190
smashed lamb wraps		50
spiced chicken kebabs & butter sauce		82
tear & share flatbread	V	176
yoghurt pasta salad	V	106

For a quick reference list of all the vegetarian, vegan, dairy-free and gluten-free recipes in this book, visit:
jamieoliver.com/BBQ/special-diets

The Jamie Oliver collection

1. The Naked Chef *1999*
2. The Return of the Naked Chef *2000*
3. Happy Days with the Naked Chef *2001*
4. Jamie's Kitchen *2002*
5. Jamie's Dinners *2004*
6. Jamie's Italy *2005*
7. Cook with Jamie *2006*
8. Jamie at Home *2007*
9. Jamie's Ministry of Food *2008*
10. Jamie's America *2009*
11. Jamie Does . . . *2010*
12. Jamie's 30-Minute Meals *2010*
13. Jamie's Great Britain *2011*
14. Jamie's 15-Minute Meals *2012*
15. Save with Jamie *2013*
16. Jamie's Comfort Food *2014*
17. Everyday Super Food *2015*
18. Super Food Family Classics *2016*
19. Jamie Oliver's Christmas Cookbook *2016*
20. 5 Ingredients – Quick & Easy Food *2017*
21. Jamie Cooks Italy *2018*
22. Jamie's Friday Night Feast Cookbook *2018*
23. Veg *2019*
24. 7 Ways *2020*
25. Together *2021*
26. ONE *2022*
27. 5 Ingredients Mediterranean *2023*
28. Simply Jamie *2024*
29. Easy Air Fryer *2025*
30. Eat Yourself Healthy *2025*
31. BBQ *2026*

Hungry for more?

For handy nutrition advice, as well as videos, features, hints, tricks and tips on all sorts of different subjects, loads of brilliant recipes, plus much more, check out

JAMIEOLIVER.COM

PENGUIN MICHAEL JOSEPH

UK | USA | CANADA | IRELAND | AUSTRALIA | INDIA | NEW ZEALAND | SOUTH AFRICA

Penguin Michael Joseph is part of the Penguin Random House group of companies whose addresses can be found at global.penguinrandomhouse.com

Penguin Michael Joseph, Penguin Random House UK,
One Embassy Gardens, 8 Viaduct Gardens, London SW11 7BW

penguin.co.uk

First published 2026

001

Copyright © Jamie Oliver, 2026

Recipe photography copyright © Jamie Oliver Enterprises Limited, 2026

© 2007 P22 Underground Pro Demi. All Rights Reserved, P22 Type Foundry, Inc.

The moral right of the author has been asserted

Photography by David Loftus

Design by Jamie Oliver Limited

Penguin Random House values and supports copyright. Copyright fuels creativity, encourages diverse voices, promotes freedom of expression and supports a vibrant culture. Thank you for purchasing an authorized edition of this book and for respecting intellectual property laws by not reproducing, scanning or distributing any part of it by any means without permission. You are supporting authors and enabling Penguin Random House to continue to publish books for everyone. No part of this book may be used or reproduced in any manner for the purpose of training artificial intelligence technologies or systems. In accordance with Article 4(3) of the DSM Directive 2019/790, Penguin Random House expressly reserves this work from the text and data mining exception

Colour reproduction by Altaimage Ltd

Printed in Germany by Mohn Media

The authorized representative in the EEA is Penguin Random House Ireland,
Morrison Chambers, 32 Nassau Street, Dublin D02 YH68

A CIP catalogue record for this book is available from the British Library

ISBN: 978–0–241–79707–5

Penguin Random House is committed to a sustainable future for our business, our readers and our planet. This book is made from Forest Stewardship Council® certified paper